Contents

Chapter 1
Getting Started

Many of you may be completely new to the world of computers. If this is the case, there is nothing to worry about. You should find this book clear and easy to follow!

This first chapter will introduce you to the package you will be using in the book, as well as covering some basic tasks such as typing, correcting mistakes and saving your work.

The package that you will be using is **Microsoft Word**, one of many different **word processing** packages. To begin working with it, you will need to load it:

 Load **Microsoft Word**. You can do this in one of two ways:

 Either double-click the **Word** icon

 Or click **Start** at the bottom left of the screen. Click on **Programs**, then click

The opening screen

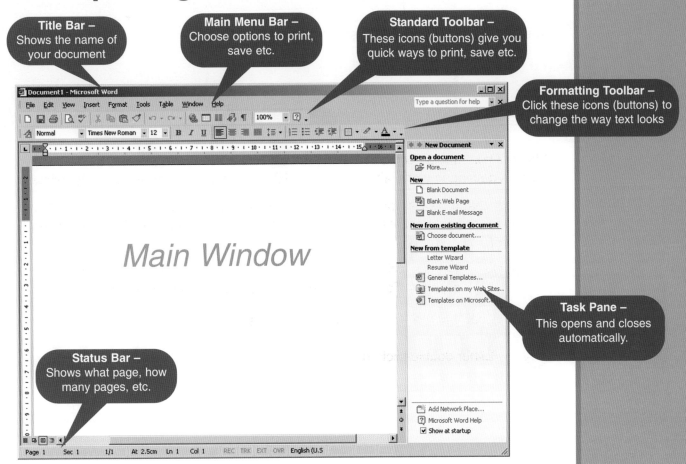

Figure 1.1: The opening screen

The **Title Bar** shows the name of your document, which might be, for example, a story or letter. If you have not given it a name yet, it will say 'Document 1' or perhaps 'Document 2' if this is your second story since you started **Microsoft Word** in this chapter.

The **Main Menu Bar** has lots of options for you to choose from. You'll be using it when you need to print or save your story.

The **Standard Toolbar** has a number of **buttons** with little pictures called **icons** which are sometimes clicked instead of choosing from the main menu.

The **Formatting Toolbar** has icons which let you change the way your text looks – for example, making the letters bigger or smaller.

The **Main Window** is the area of the screen in which you type.

The **Status Bar** shows what page you are on and how many pages there are in the document.

The **Task Pane** opens and closes automatically depending on what you are doing. You can close the Task pane at any time by clicking the **Close** icon (**X**) in its top right-hand corner.

The Keyboard

Your keyboard will look like this:

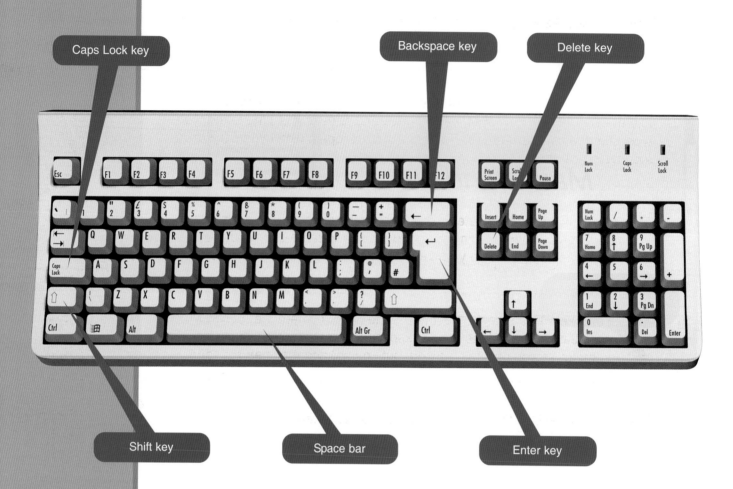

Figure 1.2: The keyboard

Some of the keys have been labelled on the diagram:

ⓘ The **Space Bar**

ⓘ The **Shift** key. As long as you hold this down, all the letters you type will be in capitals.

⬆

ⓘ The **Caps Lock** key. If you want a whole sentence to be in capitals, you can use the **Caps Lock** key. Just press it once and release it. All the letters you type after that will be capitals. Press **Caps Lock** again when you want to stop typing capitals.

Caps
Lock

ⓘ The **Backspace** key. This deletes the letter to the left of where the cursor is flashing. If you are typing something and press a wrong letter, pressing **Backspace** will delete it and you can then type the right letter. Very useful!

Backspace

←

ⓘ The **Delete** key. This deletes the letter to the right of where the cursor is flashing. It is not as useful as the Backspace key for correcting mistakes that you make as you are going along, but you will find it comes in useful.

Delete

ⓘ The **Enter** key – Use this when you want to go to a new line.

Enter

↵

Tip:
There are two **Enter** keys on the keyboard – one marked with a bent arrow and the other marked 'Enter'. They both do exactly the same thing. People who are typing lists of numbers find it easier to use the key near the numbers, while those using the main part of the keyboard to type text would probably prefer the one near the letters.

Starting to type

 Type the sentence **I have lost my watch.**

The pointer, cursor and insertion point

As you move the mouse around, the pointer moves around the screen. The pointer looks different depending on where it is on the screen.

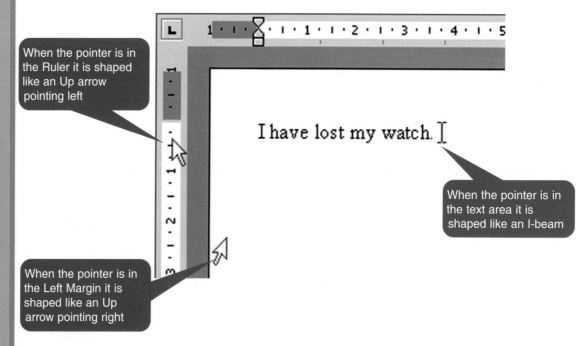

Figure 1.3: Pointer shapes

If you click in different places in and around your text, the flashing vertical line (called the **cursor**) appears in different places. It marks the **insertion point** – that is, the point at which text will be inserted when you start to type.

 Position the pointer at the beginning of the line. Take care that the pointer is the **I-beam** shape – not an arrow shape – before clicking.

▶ Type **Excuse me.** followed by a space. Now your text should say

Excuse me. I have lost my watch.

▶ Position the cursor at the end of the text and type a space followed by

Could you please tell me the time?

Now your text should say

Excuse me. I have lost my watch. Could you please tell me the time?

Sometimes, you may accidentally have the insertion point in the wrong place when you press **Enter** to start a new line. For example, if the insertion point is in the middle of the word **have** when you press **Enter**, you will end up with

Excuse me. I ha

ve lost my watch. Could you please tell me the time?

To recover from this, simply press the **Backspace** key to remove the offending **Enter**. Try it!

▶ From the Main Menu bar select **File**. Then click **Close**. You will be asked: **Do you want to save the changes to Document 1?** Click **No**.

Tip:
If your text now says
Excuse me. my watch.
you are in **Overtype** mode. Press the **Insert** key once to return to **Insert** mode and enter the missing letters.

Tip:
If you click below your text, the insertion point appears at the end of the text. If you want to insert some text further down the page you can double-click with the left mouse button where you want to insert the text and the insertion point will move there for you.
Double-clicking in the middle of text selects the nearest word.

Project: Make a list of people to invite to a meal

You are planning to celebrate your birthday by taking some friends out to a restaurant, but you have restricted yourself to 10 people.

Opening a new document

 Open a new **Word** document if you don't already have one on the screen. To do this, choose **File**, **New** from the Main Menu bar. A Task pane like this will appear, giving you various choices for the document you want to open.

Tip:
A quick way of displaying a new document is to click the **New Blank Document** button on the Standard toolbar.

 Choose the option **New**, **Blank Document** from the Task pane and your new page will appear.

Figure 1.4: Opening a new document

Entering the names

▶ Try typing a list of names. Press **Enter** after each name and type the next name on a new line. For example;

Debbie
Kirk
Anma
Athos
Paul
Sarah
Naz
Dale
Marita

▶ You have only 9 names on the list above. Insert a new name in the middle of your list to make it up to 10.

▶ You may see a wavy red line under some of the names on your list. This means either that you have misspelt the name or that the computer does not recognise it. (It is also used to show errors in punctuation such as forgetting to insert a space after a full stop.)

In the list above, the computer will fail to recognise the names of **Athos**, **Naz** and **Marita**. However, the name **Anma** has been misspelt. It is supposed to be **Anna**.

▶ Move the insertion point by clicking the mouse after the **m** in **Anma**. Use the **Backspace** key to remove the letter and replace it with the correct one by typing in an **n**. Alternatively, you could make an insertion point before the **m** and use the **Delete** key to delete the incorrect letter before inserting the correct one.

▶ Experiment!

Tip:
If you want to add a new name after **Paul** in your list, you need to click the mouse when the pointer is at the end of **Paul** to make an insertion point. Then you can press **Enter** to go to a new line and you are ready to type the new name.

Saving your work

If you want to keep your work, so that you are able to add to it or change it at any time, you must keep it safe in a **file** on a disk. (This is called **saving a file**.)

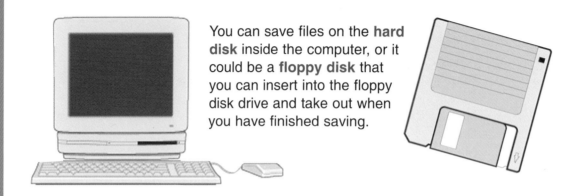

You can save files on the **hard disk** inside the computer, or it could be a **floppy disk** that you can insert into the floppy disk drive and take out when you have finished saving.

 Click **File**, **Save** on the Main Menu bar.

You'll see a screen rather like the one below. (It probably won't have as many documents on it as this though…)

Tip:
Files are held in folders which may contain other folders.

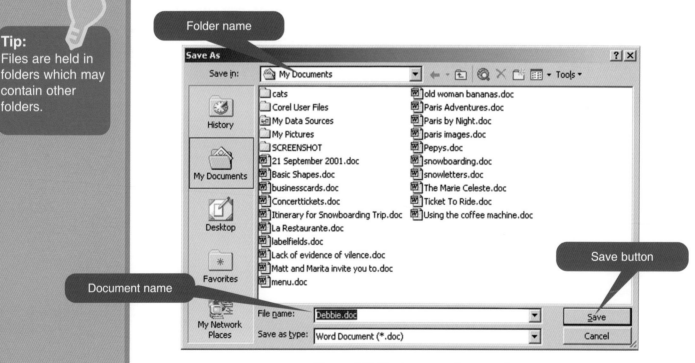

Figure 1.5: Saving your document

Word guesses a name for your file, which will be the first word or first few words you typed. The name appears in the **File name** box. The file name will be highlighted to show that it is selected ready for you to change it if you want to.

 Type a new file name. Choose a short name that will remind you of what the file contains. like **Meal**.

Microsoft Word will add a full stop and the three letters **doc** to the name you choose. This shows that it is a document created using **Microsoft Word.**

You will be given the choice of which folder you wish to save your document in. In Figure 1.5 the document will be saved in a folder called My Documents.

 Click the **Save** button. This saves your document and automatically closes the dialogue box. —————

 Close your document by selecting **File**, **Close** from the Main Menu bar.

Chapter 2
Choosing a Format

This chapter will introduce ways of altering the appearance of the text by changing its typeface or font. You will also discover how to move around your document and use new ways of selecting text so that you can change it using the buttons on the Formatting toolbar.

You may not like this Times New Roman font very much…

…and so would prefer something decorative, such as Viner Hand ITC

Fonts

Font is an alternative word for **typeface**. Both words describe the actual shape of the letters that appear on the screen when you are typing. Fonts have different names like **Times New Roman**, **Arial**, and **Comic Sans MS**.

 Open a new Word document by clicking the **New Blank Document** button on the Standard toolbar.

Look at the Formatting toolbar. The name and size of the **default font** are shown – this is the font that **Microsoft Word** will choose for you automatically, before you change it to whatever you wish.

Tip:
Word will also provide you with a default page size, document name etc.

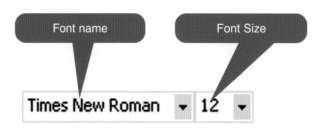

Font name   Font Size

Times New Roman   ▾   12   ▾

Figure 2.1

Project: Design a poster for a gig

You are going to use different font styles, sizes and colours to design a poster to advertise a gig. The finished poster is shown below – but don't start typing yet. Follow the instructions in the rest of this chapter!

Saturday 13th April

At the Cambridge Corn Exchange

The Journey

In Concert

Let us make a change
The eternal dream
Weight in gold

And more…

Performance begins at 7.30pm

Figure 2.2: The completed poster

Formatting the text

There are two ways in which you can format your text:

1. If you are certain of how you want your text, you may decide to choose **font style**, **size**, **colour** and **alignment** before you start typing.

2. Alternatively, you can type the text onto the page first, and then format it as you wish. If you are not sure of how you want your text to look, this gives you the opportunity to play around with different fonts.

You are going to use the first of these methods in creating your poster.

Beginning the poster

 Start by changing the font to **Arial**. To do this, click the down arrow beside the Font name box and a list of fonts will be displayed.

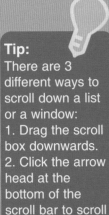
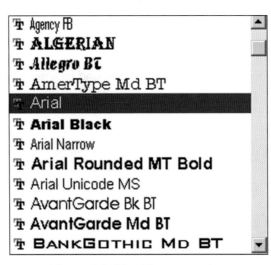

Figure 2.3: The Font name box

(The list of fonts on your computer may not be exactly the same as the one shown above.)

 Click on **Arial** to select it as your font.

`36 ▾` Click the arrow by the **Font size** box. Scroll down the list of sizes and choose a large font size – for example **36**.

You can decide whether you want your text on the left of the page, on the right of the page or in the centre.

The first five lines of the poster will have the text **centred**.

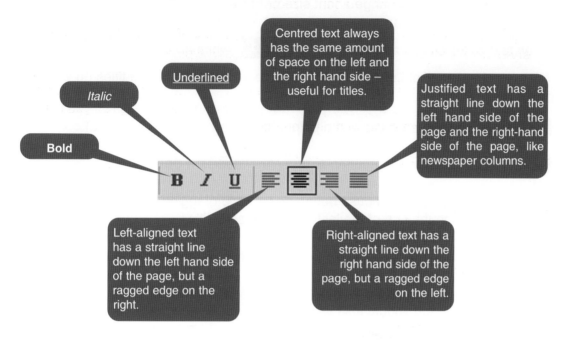

Figure 2.4: Formatting buttons

Click the **Center** button. It will look pressed in when **selected** – as in the picture above.

Click the **Center** button. It will look pressed in when **selected** – as in the picture above.

Type **Saturday 13th April** and then press **Enter** twice – this creates a more spacious effect on your poster.

Now click the **Bold** button to select it – it should look pressed in like the **Center** button.

Change the font style to *ITC Zapf Chancery* and the font size to **48**. Type the next section of the poster, *At the Cambridge Corn Exchange*. Press **Enter** twice.

Change the font size to **72** and the font style to **Times New Roman** before typing in the name of the band that is playing, **The Journey**. Press **Enter**.

Change the font size to **28** and Italic. Type **In Concert**.

Press **Enter** twice and change the font back to **Arial**, font size **28**. Also, de-select the **Bold** button and the **Italic** button by clicking them and revert to left alignment by clicking the **Align Left** button. Now you can type in the list of song titles. The line **And more…** at the end of the list of song titles should be in font size **20**. Leave some more blank space by pressing **Enter** four times.

Finally click the **Align Right** button and type **Performance begins at 7.30pm** in **Arial**, size **26**.

Tip:
If you are unsure as to what any toolbar button does, simply move the pointer over it and a tip will appear informing you of its function.

Reminder:
Copy the song titles from Figure 2.2.

Selecting text

Sometimes you want to change a font size or make text bold after you have typed it. Before you can make changes to existing text, you must **select** it.

When text is selected, it shows up **highlighted**, white on a black background.

You are going to select **Let us make a change** and the other song titles on your poster.

▶ Use the mouse to move the pointer to the left of the first letter (**L**).

▶ Click the left mouse button to move the **insertion point**.

▶ Then hold the left mouse button down while dragging down and across until you reach the end of the last line of the song titles.

▶ Release the button and the text should stay white in a black background.

▶ Click anywhere in the window away from your selected text. It is now de-selected, and should lose its black background and return to normal text.

Reminder:
The **insertion point** marks the point at which text will appear when you start typing.

Tip:
De-select is the opposite of **select**. A button that is selected looks pressed in. Clicking it for a second time de-selects it and restores it to its original appearance. When **text** is selected, it is highlighted. When you de-select it by clicking away from it, the highlighting disappears.

Making changes to the text format

Once your text is selected, you are able to make whatever changes to it you would like.

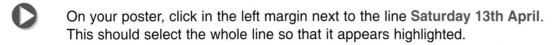 On your poster, click in the left margin next to the line **Saturday 13th April**. This should select the whole line so that it appears highlighted.

▶ Choose a different font style for this line, such as *Comic Sans MS*.

▶ Click away from it to de-select it. The highlighting should disappear.

▶ Experiment with changing the font style, font size and alignment until you are happy with the format of the text in your poster.

Once you have finished making changes to the format of your poster, you may want to see how the whole thing looks. To do this, you will need to **zoom out**, and this can be achieved by using the **Zoom** button at the end of the Standard toolbar.

▶ Click on the arrow on the right hand side of the **Zoom** button. You will be given a list of sizes to choose from. To **zoom out**, you need to select a smaller size.

▶ Select **50%** or **25%** to zoom out so that you can see the whole poster. ———
Alternatively, you can just click in the box and enter in a value yourself, such as **40%** or **33%**.

▶ If you have selected your page size by entering in your own value, then you must press **Enter** for the page size to be altered on the screen.

Tip:
If you wish to cancel the last change you have made to your text, press the **Undo** button.

Pressing it twice will undo the previous two changes, and so on.
You can reinstate the changes by pressing the **Redo** button.

| 50% | ▼ |

Adding Colour

The button on the far right of the Formatting toolbar is the one that is used for setting the colour of your text. Of course, if you don't have a colour printer, it won't show up when you print your poster.

▶ Select the lines of your text that you want to colour. Click the arrow on the right hand side of the **Font Color** button and a selection of coloured squares will appear for you to choose from. Click on one of them to select the colour of your choice.

▶ You may now use this to colour as many lines of your poster as you wish.

Save and print

▶ Click **File** on the Main Menu bar and then click **Save**.

▶ Choose a file name – e.g. **The Journey Poster** – and ensure that you are saving in the right folder.

▶ When you are ready to print off your design, click the **Print** button on the Standard toolbar.

▶ Click **File** on the Main Menu bar and then **Close** to close your document.

Chapter 3
More about Fonts

Now you are ready to type a longer piece of text and alter its appearance.

A battle of wits

Here's a short anecdote about two famous men from the early twentieth century. Read it through first. You will be using it to practise entering and changing text.

GBS – Out-Shawed

The playwright George Bernard Shaw was renowned for his disparaging remarks and once complained that "The drama critic leaves no turn unstoned". He sent Winston Churchill two tickets for the first night of his latest play, with the message "Bring a friend – if you have one". Churchill replied "Thank you very much for the tickets. Unfortunately I am unable to come to the first night but would like to come to the second – if you have one".

Adapted from *'The Wit & Wisdom of Winston Churchill'*.

Figure 3.1

Types of font

There are two basic types of font, called **Serif** and **Sans Serif**. A serif is the little tail at the top and bottom of each letter.

This is written in a Serif font called Times New Roman

This is written in a Sans Serif font called Arial

Taken from the French for '**without Serif**', **Sans Serif** fonts are very clear and are used in places where text needs to be clear and easy to read, such as road signs.

Serif fonts are more often used for large amounts of text that will be read quickly, such as in newspapers or books. The serifs 'lead your eye' from one word to the next.

You should not use too many different fonts on a page – it can end up looking a bit of a mess.

Font Sizes

Font sizes are measured in **points**. 6 point is about the smallest font you can read without the aid of a magnifying glass.

This is 6 point Times New Roman

This is 12 point Times New Roman

This is 24 point Times New Roman

This is 48 point

Typing the text

▶ If you don't already have one on the screen, open a new **Word** document.

▶ Change the **font size** to **14** by clicking the arrow to the right of the Font Size box and selecting **14**.

▶ Type the headline – which you can make **Bold** if you wish - and the first sentence of the story. Remember to press **Enter** twice after the headline, but do not press it at the end of a line. **Word** will automatically go to a new line when it has reached the end of the previous one.

More on selecting text

You have already learnt one way of selecting text in the previous chapter – here is another way that is more useful when you want to select whole lines of text in a longer document:

▶ Move the pointer to the left margin beside your headline. The pointer should appear as a left-pointing up arrow.

▶ Hold the left mouse button down and drag the mouse down the left margin until all of your text is selected.

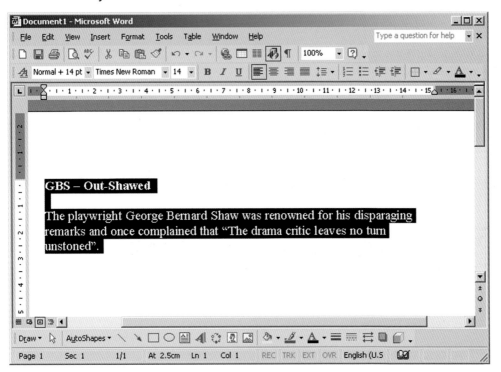

Figure 3.2: Selected text

You may also select non-adjacent lines – that is, lines that do not appear next to each other in the text:

▶ Use either of the methods of selecting you have learnt to select the headline of your story.

▶ When the first line is highlighted, release the left hand button on the mouse and move down to a line further down in the story.

Ctrl

▶ While holding down the **Ctrl** key in the bottom left of your keyboard, select the line further down in the story. This should now be selected as well as the headline. You have now selected non-adjacent lines.

▶ To de-select these lines, just click anywhere else in the text, as before.

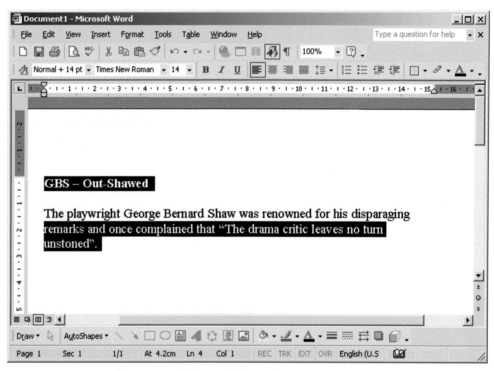

Figure 3.3: Selected lines of non-adjacent text

Typing and adjusting the rest of the story

▶ Enter the rest of the story and the last line.

▶ Select the last line and make it **Bold**.

I

▶ Select the words 'The Wit & Wisdom of Winston Churchill' and make them **Italic**.

Justified text

Text is **justified** when it goes straight down both the left and right margins. At the moment, your text will be **left-aligned**. Books and newspapers often use justified text.

▶ Select the whole of your text.

▶ Click the **Justify** button on the Formatting toolbar.

GBS – Out-Shawed

The playwright George Bernard Shaw was renowned for his disparaging remarks and once complained that "The drama critic leaves no turn unstoned". He sent Winston Churchill two tickets for the first night of his latest play, with the message "Bring a friend – if you have one". Churchill replied "Thank you very much for the tickets. Unfortunately I am unable to come to the first night but would like to come to the second – if you have one".

Adapted from *'The Wit & Wisdom of Winston Churchill'*.

Figure 3.4: Justified text

Saving and printing your work

▶ Save your article, giving it a suitable name.

▶ When you are ready to print, click the **Print** button on the Standard toolbar.

▶ Close the file.

Chapter 4
Using Graphics

You can add pictures, scanned photographs or cartoons to your documents.

There are some **clip art** images stored with Microsoft Word. You can also buy CDs with thousands of pictures and graphics of all kinds.

Project: Write an article and illustrate it

You are going to write a short article about the age-old mystery of the *Marie Celeste* and use clip art to illustrate it.

 ▶ Open a new document by clicking the button on the Standard toolbar.

▶ Type the heading *The Marie Celeste*.

▶ Make the heading **Vivaldi** font, size **20**, **Bold** and **Centred**.

▶ Type the lines in the box below using **Times New Roman** font, size **14**, **Aligned Left**, and not **Bold**. Make the ship names that are mentioned **Italic**.

The Marie Celeste

The *Marie Celeste* was launched in Nova Scotia in 1860, with the original name "*Amazon*". Over a period of 10 years she was involved in several accidents at sea and passed through a number of owners. Eventually she turned up at a New York salvage auction where she was purchased for $3,000. After extensive repairs she was put under American registry and renamed "*Marie Celeste*".

Figure 4.1

 ▶ Press **Enter** twice so that you have two blank lines at the end of the document.

Importing clip art

Clip art is a collection of pictures and drawings that have been drawn by professional artists and collected together for other people to use. **Microsoft Word** comes with a small collection of clip art.

 Click **Insert** on the Main Menu bar. Select **Picture** and then **Clip Art**.

A Task pane will appear on the right of the screen (see Figure 4.2).

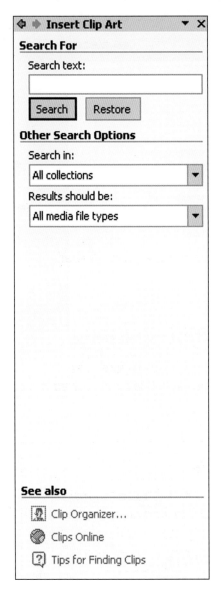

To accompany your article, you can import a picture of a 19th century ship.

 Type **ship** into the box under the heading Search Text and then click on the **Search** button underneath it.

A selection of relevant pictures will appear in the Task pane.

 Scroll down until you find the ship below.

Figure 4.2: The Clip Art Task pane

 Click on this picture. The ship will be inserted into your document.

 Close the Clip Art Task pane by clicking on the cross in the top right hand corner of the Task pane.

When you want to make changes to your graphic, it will be better if you can see more of the page on screen.

`75%` ▼

▶ Click the arrow beside the **Zoom** button and select **75%**.

Now your document should look like the one below:

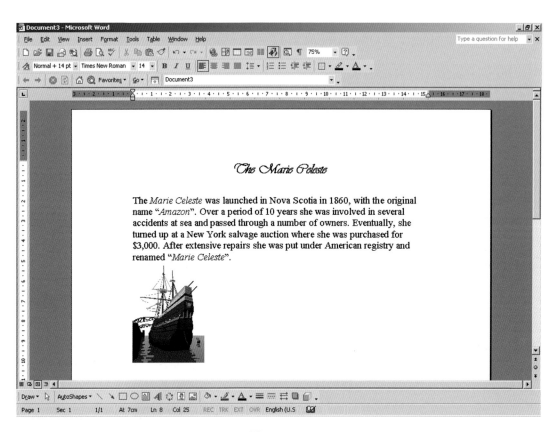

Figure 4.3

Selecting the graphic

If you wish to change the graphic (picture) in any way, you first need to select it.

▶ Click anywhere inside the graphic. Small squares and an outline should appear, surrounding it. These are called **handles**. When the handles are visible, the graphic is **selected**.

▶ Click anywhere away from the graphic and the handles will disappear again.

Figure 4.4

Changing the size of a graphic

You can make the graphic bigger or smaller without changing its proportions by dragging any of the corner handles.

▶ Make sure the graphic is selected so that the handles are visible.

▶ Move the pointer over the bottom right handle until it is shaped like a diagonal two-headed arrow.

▶ Click and hold down the left mouse button. The pointer will change to a cross-hair.

▶ Drag inwards and upwards to make the graphic smaller. A dotted rectangle shows how big the graphic will be when you release the mouse button.

▶ Alternatively, drag outwards and downwards to increase the size of the graphic.

▶ Experiment with this until you are happy with it. The graphic should be roughly one third the width of a line of text (see Figure 4.3).

Moving a graphic

Once you have imported your graphic, it would be convenient if you were able to move it anywhere you wanted with the mouse. However, when the handles are black this is not possible.

▶ Click anywhere inside your ship with the right hand mouse button. A shortcut (pop-up) menu will appear.

Figure 4.5: The shortcut menu

▶ Click **Format Picture**, near the bottom of the shortcut menu.

▶ The **Format Picture** window appears. Click the tab labelled **Layout**.

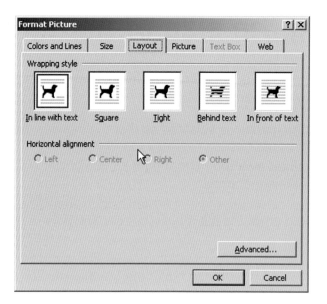

Figure 4.6: The Format Picture window

The **wrapping style** is now **In line with text**, which means that the graphic is an actual part of the text so can't be moved about.

 Click the **Square** wrapping style, then click **OK**.

Figure 4.7

The ship now has white round handles.

 Click anywhere in the graphic and hold down the left mouse button. You will find that you can drag it about the page. Again, a dotted line appears which indicates where the graphic will move to when you release the mouse button.

There will also be a *green* circle, located above the top of the graphic. This is the **Rotate** tool.

 Move the pointer near the **Rotate** tool and it should become a circular arrow surrounding it. Click now and you can rotate the graphic through any angle.

 Experiment with moving and rotating the graphic until you are happy with it.

Copying and pasting graphics

You may want more than one ship in your article – let's say you want three. Instead of having to insert the graphic three times, you can copy and paste:

▶ Click anywhere in the ship to select it.

▶ Click the **Copy** button on the Standard toolbar.

▶ Now click the **Paste** button on the Standard toolbar. This will create a second ship.

▶ Click **Paste** again to create your third ship. You can now move the ships anywhere you like on the page by dragging them.

Distorting a graphic

Distorting a graphic means changing its shape. This will happen if you drag one of the side handles.

▶ Space out your three ships on the page so that they do not overlap – select each one in turn by clicking away from the handles then drag it to a new place.

▶ Select a ship and drag the middle left handle to the left. The ship will become wider.

▶ Select another ship and drag the bottom middle handle downwards. This time the ship should become much taller.

Your page may now look something like the one below. If your ships are now too large to fit on a single line, just make them smaller.

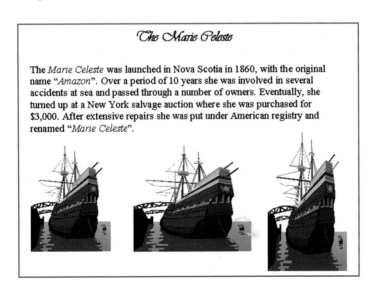

Figure 4.8

Placing text around a graphic

When you move your ships around the page the text may move too. This will happen when you move a ship *up into* the text.

Sometimes you may want to have writing next to, around or even on top of your graphic.

To practise this, you will only need your original ship.

 Select one of the distorted ships, and press the **Delete** key. Repeat this to remove the other one.

 Select the remaining ship and move it about in and around the text.

When you deselect the ship you should see that the text flows or **wraps** around the shape of the graphic.

The Marie Celeste

The *Marie Celeste* was launched in Nova Scotia in 1860, with the original name "Amazon". Over a period of 10 years she was involved in several accidents at sea and   passed through a number of owners. Eventually,   she turned up at a New York salvage auction where   she was purchased for $3,000. After extensive   repairs she was put under American registry and   renamed "Marie Celeste".

Figure 4.9

You might want the text to be on one side of the graphic only.

 Select the ship and move it to the right-hand side of the text.

The Marie Celeste

The *Marie Celeste* was launched in Nova Scotia in 1860, with the original name "*Amazon*". Over a period of 10 years she was involved in several accidents at sea and passed through a number of owners. Eventually, she turned up at a New York salvage auction where she was purchased for $3,000. After extensive repairs she was put under American registry and renamed "*Marie Celeste*".

Figure 4.10

Ordering graphics

 Copy the ship and press the **Paste** button several times to create several ships.

Figure 4.11

 Drag the ships separately under the text.

 Make some of them smaller.

To get the smaller ships to seem furthest away, they need to be behind the larger ones.

 Right-click a ship that you want at the back and from the shortcut menu select **Order**.

 Select **Send to Back**.

 Bring the larger ships to the front by right-clicking them, selecting **Order**, and then either **Bring to Front** or **Bring Forward**.

Grouping graphics

Sometimes it is useful to group individual graphics into one graphic so that you can move everything together.

 Delete some ships until you have three left. Position them so that they do not overlap.

 On the **Drawing** toolbar at the bottom of the screen, click the **Select Objects** tool.

 Select all three of your ships by dragging diagonally across them.

 Right-click anywhere inside one of the ships and select **Grouping**, then **Group**.

Tip:
If the **Drawing** toolbar is not at the bottom of the screen, you can bring it onto the screen by clicking on **View** on the Main Menu bar, then **Toolbars**, and then **Drawing**.

You will see that the three ships are now surrounded by just one set of handles. You can now move them as one single graphic.

Figure 4.12

Finishing the story

▶ Press **Enter** twice at the end of the text to leave some space.

▶ Type the following text:

The new captain of *Marie Celeste* was Benjamin Briggs, 37, a master with three previous commands. On November 7, 1872 the ship departed New York with Captain Briggs, his wife, young daughter and a crew of eight. The ship was cargoed with 1700 barrels of raw American alcohol and bound for Genoa, Italy. Four weeks later, it was found by the crew of another ship, the *Dei Gratia*, floating and completely abandoned. The only life boat had been launched, and yet the ship, apart from some minor damage to the compass, was in perfect shape. Indeed, legend has it that below decks the tables were still set for dinner, food lying uneaten by the vanished crew. The captain, his family and the crew were never seen again.

Saving and printing

▶ Save your article as **Marie Celeste**, and print it using the **Print** button on the Standard toolbar.

▶ Close your document.

Chapter 5
Longer Documents

In this chapter you will be creating a longer document, going over more than one page.

Learning to type

Most of us are 'two-fingered typists', which means that we only normally use two fingers on the keyboard. Naturally, you will be able to type much faster if you learn to type properly, without looking at the keyboard – this is called **touch-typing**.

This book can't teach you to touch-type – if you wish to learn this there are lots of CDs available.

Figure 5.1: The correct rest position for the four fingers of each hand

If you pause while typing the fingers of your left hand should rest on **ASDF**. The fingers of your right hand should rest on **JKL;** with the little finger on the ;. Then you're ready to type with all eight fingers, using your thumbs for the space bar.

On the top row of letters on the keyboard, your little fingers should type the **Q** and the **P**. When typing from the bottom row of letters, your little fingers should be typing the **Z** and the **/**. Even if you are a two-fingered typist, you should still give it a try.

Writing your text

You are going to type a few entries from the diary of Samuel Pepys, a famous English diarist whose writing covers events such as the Great Plague and the Great Fire of London. Don't worry if you find some of the style or the spellings odd – the English language in which Pepys wrote (in the 17th century) is slightly different from our modern English.

 Make sure you have a new document open. Change the font size to size **14**, and type in the following text. (For the purposes of this chapter you need only type the first sentence of each entry.)

2nd September 1666

Some of our maids sitting up late last night to get things ready against our feast today, Jane called us up, about 3 in the morning, to tell us of a great fire they saw in the City. So I rose, and slipped on my nightgown and went to her window and thought it to be on the back side of Markelane at the furthest; but being unused to such fires as fallowed, I thought it far enough off, and so went to bed again and to sleep. About 7 rose again and there looked out at the window and saw the fire not so much as it was, and further off. By and by Jane comes and tells me that she hears above 300 houses have been burned down tonight by the fire we saw, and that it was now burning down by London Bridge.

4th September 1666

This night Mrs. Turner and her husband supped with my wife and I at night in the office, upon a shoulder of mutton from the cook's, without any napkin or anything, in a sad manner but were merry. Only, now and then walking into the garden and saw how horridly the sky looks, all on a fire in the night, was enough to put us out of our wits; and endeed it was extremely dreadfull – for it looks just as if it was at us, and the whole heaven on fire.

5th September 1666

I lay down in the office again upon W. Hewer's quilt, being mighty weary and sore in my feet with going till I was hardly able to stand. About 2 in the morning my wife calls me up and tells of new Cryes of "Fyre!" But Lord, what a sad sight it was by moonlight to see the whole City almost on fire – that you might see it plain at Woolwich, as if you were by it. There when I came, I find the gates shut, but no guard kept at all; which troubled me, because of discourses now begun that there is plot in it and that the French had done it.

You have typed extracts from the diary of Samuel Pepys, describing his thoughts and movements in reaction to the beginning of the Great Fire of London in 1666. They were written on 3 separate dates, which form the headings of the respective entries.

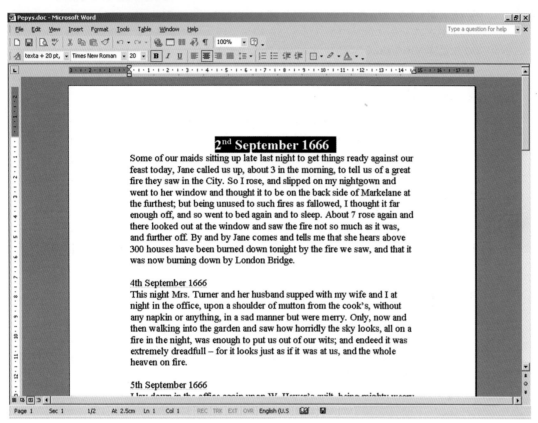

▶ Save your file, giving it a suitable name like **Pepys**.

▶ Go to the first date/heading of your text. Select it by clicking in the margin to the left of it, and make it size **20**, **Bold** and **Centred**. It will look like this while it is selected:

Figure 5.2

▶ Make the other dates the same style as the first one.

You need more space between the date and the first line of each entry.

▶ Click at the end of the first date.

▶ Press **Enter**.

▶ Do the same for the other two dates in your text.

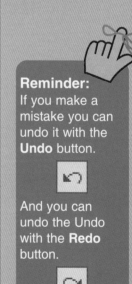

Reminder:
If you make a mistake you can undo it with the **Undo** button.

And you can undo the Undo with the **Redo** button.

Starting a new entry on a new page

It is better to start each of the entries (or maybe chapters depending on what it is you are writing) on a new page. To do this, you need to insert a **page break** just before the dates of the second and third entries.

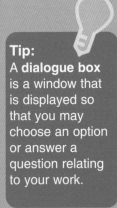

▶ Click the cursor just before the **4** in the date **4th September 1666**.

▶ From the Main Menu bar, select **Insert**, and then **Break**.

You will see a dialogue box open, like the one below.

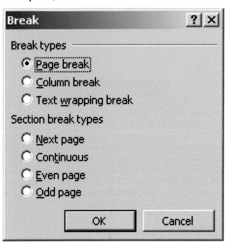

Figure 5.3: Break dialogue box

▶ **Page break** is the default selection. Since you want a page break, you can click **OK**.

▶ Insert another page break just before the date for the third entry, **5th September 1666**.

The scroll bars

You can use the **vertical scroll bar**, on the right of the screen, to move up and down your document.

To scroll up one line...
Click the **up** scroll arrow

To scroll down one line...
Click the **down** scroll arrow

To scroll up one screen...
Click **above** the scroll box

To scroll down one screen...
Click **below** the scroll box

To scroll to a specific page...
Drag the scroll box

When you click and hold down the button on the scroll bar, a **tool tip** tells you what page of your document you're on.

Up scroll arrow

Scroll box (or Thumb)

Down scroll arrow

 Practise scrolling up and down your document. Sometimes the text seems to disappear – probably because you are looking at a part of the page that is blank!

Warning:
If you have an older version of **Microsoft Word**, you may find you do not get tool tips.

Saving a second version of your document

Normally when you save a document a second time, it **overwrites** the original version – meaning that it uses the same space again and the original version is lost. However, sometimes you may want to keep two different versions.

 Select **File** from the Main Menu bar. Click **Save As**.

 Now you are able to enter in a new file name, for example **Pepys2**. You will now have two versions of his diary entries – one with the text before you did any formatting, and the other with each entry on a separate page.

 Close your document.

Chapter 6
Spelling Checker

In this chapter you will be doing more work with the article you wrote on the *Marie Celeste* in Chapter 4 and the diary entries of Samuel Pepys that you typed in the previous chapter.

 Open the document you saved as **Marie Celeste**.

The three ships should still be grouped together.

 Move the three ships so that they appear in between the two paragraphs of text – click anywhere inside any of them, and drag them into the text.

You may find that a small amount of text remains on one side of your ships.

To ensure that the text only appears above and below the graphic:

 Right-click anywhere inside the graphic.

 Select **Format Picture** from the shortcut menu, and then click on the **Layout** tab.

 Click on the **Advanced** button before selecting **Top and Bottom** from the options under the **Text Wrapping** tab. This will place text only above and below your graphic, and avoid any unwanted small amounts of text to the side.

You are going to add some more text to the end of your article.

 Position the cursor just after the full stop at the end of the final sentence, and click.

Press **Enter** twice to go to a new line and leave space in between. Then type in the following paragraph.

(There are two spelling mistakes in the text below – copy them just as they are.)

A British Board of Inquiry in Gibraltar gathered evidence and testimony from the boarding party that had discovered the Marie Celeste as a drifting derelict. Lack of evidence of vilence ruled owt piracy or foul play, but no conclusions as to the fate of the mortals aboard was forthcoming.

 Save your file. You can do it quickly by clicking the **Save** button on the Standard toolbar.

Your file will be saved with the same name it had when you opened it.

Warning:
If there is a power cut or the computer suddenly locks up for no obvious reason, you will have to turn it off and then on again, thereby losing all of the work you have done since you last saved.
This is why you should **save your work every few minutes**. This will save you much time redoing work you have already done if disaster strikes.

Checking the spelling

Your page should now look like this:

The Marie Celeste

The *Marie Celeste* was launched in Nova Scotia in 1860, with the original name "*Amazon*". Over a period of 10 years she was involved in several accidents at sea and passed through a number of owners. Eventually, she turned up at a New York salvage auction where she was purchased for $3,000. After extensive repairs she was put under American registry and renamed "*Marie Celeste*".

The new captain of *Marie Celeste* was Benjamin Briggs, 37, a master with three previous commands. On November 7, 1872 the ship departed New York with Captain Briggs, his wife, young daughter and a crew of eight. The ship was cargoed with 1700 barrels of raw American alcohol and bound for Genoa, Italy. Four weeks later, it was found by the crew of another ship, the *Dei Gratia*, floating and completely abandoned. The only life boat had been launched, and yet the ship, apart from some minor damage to the compass, was in perfect shape. Indeed, legend has it that below decks the tables were still set for dinner, food lying uneaten by the vanished crew. The captain, his family and the crew were never seen again.

A British Board of Inquiry in Gibraltar gathered evidence and testimony from the boarding party that had discovered the Marie Celeste as a drifting derelict. Lack of evidence of vilence ruled owt piracy or foul play, but no conclusions as to the fate of the mortals aboard was forthcoming.

Figure 6.1

Tip:
You will also get the red underlining if you accidentally type a word twice – for example "The cat sat sat on the mat". **Word** knows that you did not really intend to type 'sat' twice and so informs you of your mistake.

You will notice that some words in your text are underlined with a red wavy line. **Microsoft Word** has a dictionary stored on disk, and the wavy red line usually means that these words are not in it.

If the screen looks like Figure 6.1, you will see two words underlined:

vilence   owt

This is because they are misspelt.

Correcting individual words

There are several ways in which you can ask **Word** to check your spelling. You can ask it to check the whole document, or you can get it to check each word that is underlined in red. That's what we're going to do.

 Put the cursor anywhere inside the word **vilence** and right-click the mouse. A small pop-up menu will appear:

You are given the following choices:

 Decide which spelling from the menu is the correct one – in this case it is **violence** – and click it.

Word will make the correction for you.

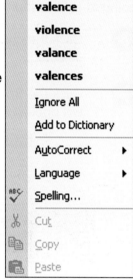

Figure 6.2

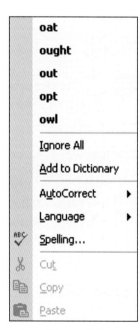

 Now right-click the word **owt**.

 Choose the correct spelling

 Save your file once you have successfully corrected both spelling mistakes in your document.

Figure 6.3

Checking the spelling of a whole document

Tip:
You may need to type some more of the text shown on page 34 if you have not typed it all.

▶ Open the diary entries of Samuel Pepys that you typed and saved in the previous chapter. It should be saved as **Pepys2**.

The entries contain some spellings that are incorrect in modern English – you are going to amend them so that they are correct present-day English.

▶ Click the cursor at the very beginning of the document. No text should be selected.

▶ Click the **Spelling and Grammar** button on the Standard toolbar. A window will appear like the one below:

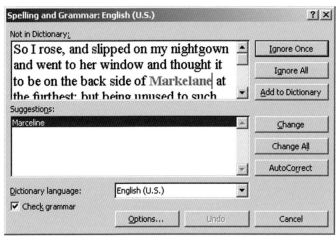

Figure 6.4

▶ The dictionary language selected is English (U.S.). Click the arrow to the right of the dictionary language box and click English (U.K.) from the options.

The first word picked out by the spell check is **Markelane**. This is a proper name and so can be ignored.

▶ Click on the **Ignore Once** button and the computer will automatically move on to the next word that it does not recognise.

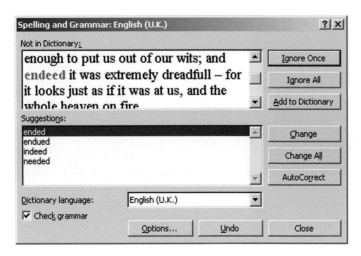

Figure 6.5

The spelling checker provides you with suggestions to replace the highlighted word. In this case the correct word is **indeed**.

  Select **indeed** from the suggestions box and click the **Change** button. The computer will move on to the next word underlined in red:

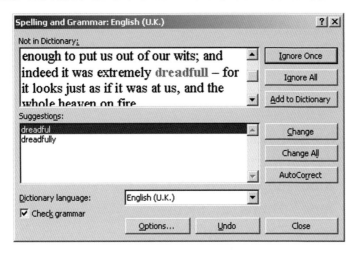

Figure 6.6

  Again you are provided with a suggestion that you want to accept – **dreadful**. Click on **Change** again to insert the correct spelling.

  Continue your spell-check until you've changed all the words that need changing – there should be two more: **Cryes** and **Fyre**.

You can't rely on **Microsoft Word** to pick up all of the mistakes you might make. For example, if in your article on the *Marie Celeste* you typed **fete** rather than **fate** in the last line, the spelling checker would not pick it up. This is because **fete** is also a word and so exists in the **Word** dictionary.

  Save your corrected diary entries using a different name – such as **Pepys3**.

  Close your document.

Chapter 7
Cut, Copy and Paste

Microsoft Word makes it very easy to copy or move text about once you have typed it.

Project: Writing the words to a rhyme

You are going to use the cut, copy and paste buttons to help you write a nursery rhyme that contains a lot of repetition.

 Copy out the first five lines of the first verse from **Old MacDonald**. Remember to press **Enter** at the end of each line.

Old MacDonald

Old MacDonald had a farm, E-I-E-I-O
And on his farm he had a cow, E-I-E-I-O
With a "moo-moo" here and a "moo-moo" there
Here a "moo" there a "moo"
Everywhere a "moo-moo"

Figure 7.1

The last line of the verse is a repetition of the first line.

You are going to use the **Copy** and **Paste** buttons to save yourself the trouble of having to write out the same line again.

Copying text

▶ Select the line **Old MacDonald had a farm, E-I-E-I-O** by clicking in the left hand margin next to the line.

▶ Click the **Copy** button on the Standard toolbar.

▶ Press **Enter** after the last line.

▶ Click at the beginning of the new blank line.

▶ Click the **Paste** button.

The line will be copied into the text.

Now type in the first five lines of the next two verses:

> Old MacDonald had a farm, E-I-E-I-O
> And on his farm he had a horse, E-I-E-I-O
> With a "neigh, neigh" here and a "neigh, neigh" there
> Here a "neigh" there a "neigh"
> Everywhere a "neigh, neigh"
>
> Old MacDonald had a farm, E-I-E-I-O
> And on his farm he had a pig, E-I-E-I-O
> With a (snort, snort) here and a (snort, snort) there
> Here a (snort) there a (snort)
>   Everywhere a (snort, snort)

Figure 7.2: Beginning the next two verses

Tip:
You will see an icon which looks like the **Paste** button appearing under your text. This is called a **smart tag**. It allows you to change the formatting of the text you have copied.

Cutting and pasting

Suppose we've made a mistake and Old MacDonald had a pig *before* he had a horse!

We can move the third verse back to become the second verse using the **Cut** button.

 Select the verse you have just typed (about the pig) by clicking in the margin to its left and dragging down.

 Click on the **Cut** button on the Standard toolbar. The selected text will disappear, but it is not lost completely: It is being stored for you.

 Now click immediately before the first line in the second verse (about the horse) and click the **Paste** button. The verse is now pasted from the clipboard into the text exactly where you want it.

Press **Enter** after your pasted verse if you need to insert another blank line.

Cutting and pasting is very useful when you are writing your own text and want to move things around.

Tip:
You have been using buttons from the Standard toolbar to **Cut**, **Copy** and **Paste**. However, if you would prefer, alternative ways are provided for you:
1. Click **Edit**, followed by **Cut**, **Copy** or **Paste** from the Main Menu bar.
2. Use the keyboard: for **Cut**, press **Ctrl + X**, for **Copy**, press **Ctrl + C**, for **Paste**, press **Ctrl + V**.

Completing the rhyme

 Now use the **Copy** and **Paste** buttons again to copy the parts of the rhyme that repeat (i.e. lines 3-5 from each verse and the last line). The completed rhyme should look something like this:

Old MacDonald

Old MacDonald had a farm, E-I-E-I-O
And on his farm he had a cow, E-I-E-I-O
With a "moo-moo" here and a "moo-moo" there
Here a "moo" there a "moo"
Everywhere a "moo-moo"
Old MacDonald had a farm, E-I-E-I-O

Old MacDonald had a farm, E-I-E-I-O
And on his farm he had a pig, E-I-E-I-O
With a (snort-snort) here and a (snort-snort) there
Here a (snort) there a (snort)
Everywhere a (snort-snort)
With a "moo-moo" here and a "moo-moo" there
Here a "moo" there a "moo"
Everywhere a "moo-moo"
Old MacDonald had a farm, E-I-E-I-O

Old MacDonald had a farm, E-I-E-I-O
And on his farm he had a horse, E-I-E-I-O
With a "neigh, neigh" here and a "neigh, neigh" there
Here a "neigh" there a "neigh"
Everywhere a "neigh, neigh"
With a (snort, snort) here and a (snort, snort) there
Here a (snort) there a (snort)
Everywhere a (snort, snort)
With a "moo-moo" here and a "moo-moo" there
Here a "moo" there a "moo"
Everywhere a "moo-moo"
Old MacDonald had a farm, E-I-E-I-O

Figure 7.3

Finding and replacing text

Suppose that after completing your lyrics, you decide that you would prefer the pig in the rhyme to **grunt** rather than **snort**.

As you can see this word appears many times and you need a quick way of changing each occurrence.

 Click at the start of the first line.

 From the Main Menu bar, select **Edit** then **Replace** (or press **Ctrl + H** on the keyboard).

You will see a dialogue box and you can type the word or phrase you want to replace, and the word or phrase to replace it with.

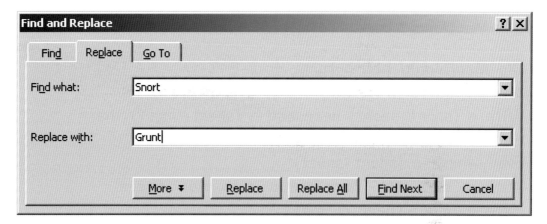

Figure 7.4: Finding and replacing text

You can get the computer to replace all occurrences, or search for them one at a time so that you can decide whether or not to replace each one. In this case you want them all replaced.

 Press the button marked **Replace All**. **Word** tells you how many words have been replaced.

Figure 7.5

Chapter 8
Drawing Tools, Bullets and Borders

In Chapter 4 you imported some clip art to help illustrate an article you were writing. In this chapter you will be drawing your own simple shapes.

The Drawing toolbar

There are two ways to display the Drawing toolbar:

▶ Click **View** from the Main Menu bar. Then select **Toolbars** and click on **Drawing** from the list of toolbars. The Drawing toolbar appears at the bottom of the screen.

Or,

▶ Click the **Drawing** button on the Standard toolbar once and the Drawing toolbar appears at the bottom of the screen. Click it again and it disappears.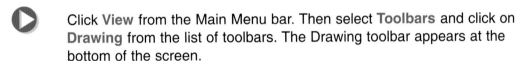

This type of button or switch is called a **toggle**. It works in the same way as the cord that turns bathroom lights on and off.

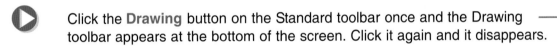

Figure 8.1: The Drawing toolbar

▶ Open a new **Word** document by clicking the **New Blank Document** button on the Standard toolbar.

▶ Make sure that the **Drawing toolbar** is displayed at the bottom of the screen.

Drawing simple shapes

▶ Type a heading at the top of the page:

Basic Shapes

▶ Click the **Rectangle** button on the Drawing toolbar. A drawing canvas appears on the screen suggesting where to create your drawing:

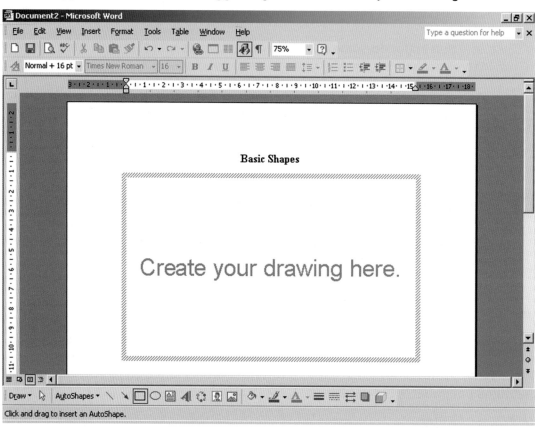

Figure 8.2: The drawing canvas

▶ De-select the drawing canvas as described. It will then disappear from the screen. You'll need to click the **Rectangle** button on the Drawing toolbar again in order to create your drawing.

You'll notice that when you click the **Rectangle** tool, the pointer on the screen changes to a cross-hair. Wherever you click now will be the top left-hand corner of the rectangle.

▶ Position the cross-hair somewhere near the insertion point on the screen. Click and hold the left mouse button down while you drag out a rectangle about the size of the one below.

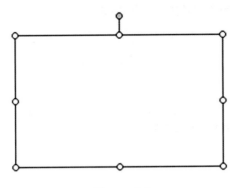

Figure 8.3

▶ You should see handles around the rectangle, showing that it is selected. If there are no handles, click anywhere within the shape to select it.

▶ Change the thickness of the line by clicking the **Line Style** button on the Drawing toolbar.

▶ Select a line thickness – say size 1.5 or 3.

▶ Now click the arrow beside the **Fill** button on the Drawing toolbar. Choose a colour to fill the rectangle.

▶ Save the document, giving it a suitable name.

Tip:
You can **change the size** of the rectangle without changing its proportions by dragging any of the corner handles.
You can **move** the rectangle by clicking anywhere inside it and dragging – taking care to keep away from the handles when doing this.
You can **change the shape** of the rectangle by dragging one of the handles in the middle of a side.

Drawing a square

▶ Click the **Rectangle** button again, but this time hold down the **Shift** key while you drag out a shape on the page. Holding down the **Shift** key ensures that the shape will be a perfect square.

▶ Change the line thickness using the **Line Style** button.

▶ Click the arrow beside the **Fill** button and fill the square with a different colour.

Basic Shapes

 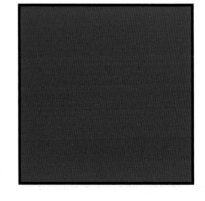

Figure 8.4

Text boxes

Next you can add labels to your shapes by placing a **text box** under each shape.

▶ Make sure that neither of your shapes is selected – click away from them if you need to.

▶ Click the **Text Box** button on the Drawing toolbar.

▶ Drag out a box under the rectangle that you have already drawn. The text box should be about the same width as the rectangle.

▶ Click inside the text box that you have just drawn. An insertion point will flash to show that you can now type text.

▶ Change the font to **Arial**, size **14**, **Bold** and **Centred** before you start typing.

▶ Type **Rectangle** (see Figure 8.5).

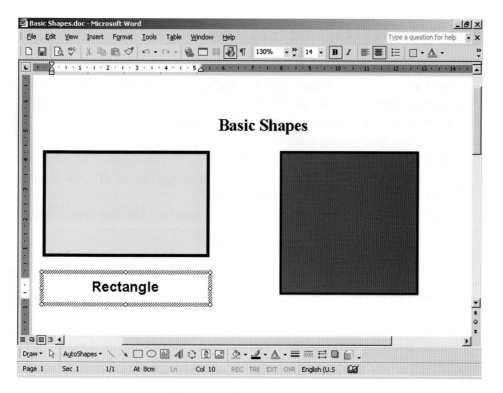

Figure 8.5: Placing a text box

Tip:
If you want to change the font size or alignment *after* you have typed the text in a text box, you must first select the text by dragging across it to highlight it. Alternatively, you can select the whole text box by clicking anywhere along its border, and then make the relevant font changes.

You can alter the size of the text box in the same way as you can change the size of any graphic – simply drag any of the handles.

When you click away from the text box, you will probably find that it has a black border around it. You may decide that you don't want this.

▶ Click anywhere on the border of your text box to select the box rather than the text inside it.

▶ Click the arrow beside the **Line Color** button on the Drawing toolbar. ———

▶ Select **No Line**.

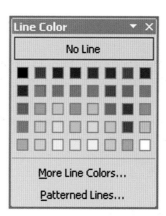

Figure 8.6: Selecting a line colour

Tip:
You are able to **change the colour** of the text in a text box by selecting the box and then clicking the arrow by the **Font Color** button on the Drawing toolbar.

▶ Repeat this process to place and label a text box underneath your square.

Placing other shapes

▶ Now place an oval shape. Colour it in the same way that you coloured the other shapes.

▶ Place a text box underneath it and type **Oval** in the text box.

▶ Place a circle by holding down **Shift** while dragging out an oval shape.

▶ Colour the circle and then label it using a text box like the one shown in Figure 8.5.

3-D shapes

You can turn a square into a cube or a circle into a cylinder.

▶ Click the **Rectangle** button on the Drawing toolbar. Place a square on the page by holding down the **Shift** key while dragging out a rectangle.

▶ With the square selected, click the **3-D** button on the far right of the Drawing toolbar.

▶ Choose one of the 3-D shapes from the options given. The first one has been chosen in Figure 8.7.

▶ Colour your cube and label it using a text box as before.

▶ Now, by following the same process with the **Oval** button, you can create and label a cylinder.

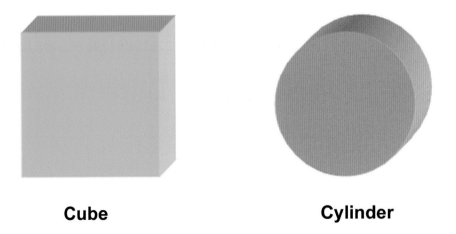

Cube   **Cylinder**

Figure 8.7: 3-D shapes

Autoshapes

Word provides you with a selection of other shapes that you can place, colour and label if you wish.

▶ Click on the **Autoshapes** button on the Drawing toolbar. A pop-up menu will appear giving you several choices.

▶ Select **Basic Shapes** and from the options that appear click on the lightning shape. Then drag out a lightning shape on your page, and colour it yellow. You may experiment with Autoshapes until you are happy creating, colouring and arranging them.

Figure 8.8: Examples of Autoshapes

Finishing touches

▶ Drag your shapes and text boxes around the page until you are happy with their arrangement.

▶ Save your work, and print it out when you are ready.

▶ Close your document.

Tip:
You can also place text in your Autoshapes. Right-click anywhere inside your shape, and choose **Add text** from the pop-up menu that appears. Then type what you want and it will appear inside your shape.

Tip:
You can move each shape and its text box as one object. To do this, select a shape. Then, holding down the **Shift** key, click on the border of the accompanying text box – this will ensure that both shape and text box are selected. Now click **Draw** on the Drawing toolbar, and click on the **Group** button. This will group together the shape and text box, enabling you to move them together.

Bullets and Borders

Finally you are going to create a poster to help with a typical office problem – working the coffee machine.

Using the coffee machine

- Put a sheet of filter paper in the coffee compartment.

- Measure coffee into filter paper – one tablespoon of coffee for each cup you are making.

- Using the scale marked on the side of the jug, fill the jug with the required amount of water.

- Pour the water into the top compartment, and place the jug on the base of the machine.

- Turn the machine on and wait for your coffee to filter through…

Figure 8.9

▶ Open a new document.

▶ Select a suitable font for the title. The one in Figure 8.9 is **Britannic Bold**, size **36**.

▶ Type the heading and make sure that it is **Centred**.

▶ Press **Enter** twice after the heading and change to a different font. The one used above is **Arial**, size **24**.

Making bullets

▶ Click the **Bullets** button on the Formatting toolbar.

▶ Type the instructions listed in Figure 8.9. Each time you press **Enter**, a bullet will automatically appear on the next line.

▶ After typing the last item in the list, press **Enter** once more.

▶ Turn off the bullets by clicking the **Bullets** button again.

▶ Select the list by either dragging across each bullet point or dragging down the left hand margin.

▶ Click the **Numbering** button. Your list should now have numbers instead of bullets.

▶ Now click the **Bullets** button again to revert back to bullets instead of numbers.

Spacing paragraphs

Every time you press **Enter**, you create a new paragraph. So, in your list, **Word** treats each separate bullet point as a separate paragraph. You can put extra space between each bullet point so that the list fills the page more neatly.

▶ If the list is not already selected, select it now.

▶ Right-click the list to display a shortcut menu.

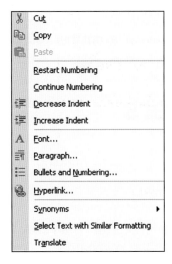

Figure 8.10

▶ Select **Paragraph...** The following window appears:

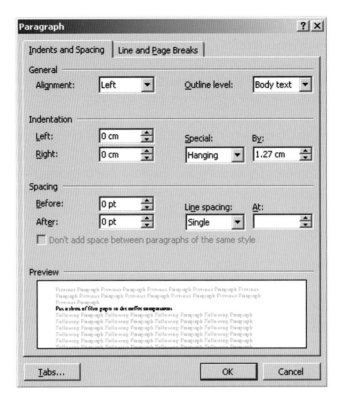

Figure 8.11

▶ In the **Spacing Before** box, click the up arrow until **12** is displayed. Click **OK**.

▶ If that is not enough spacing to comfortably fill your page, try again. You could try increasing the **Spacing Before** to size **18**, or alternatively you could insert some **Spacing After** each paragraph using the Spacing After box.

▶ Experiment until you have a layout that you are happy with.

Placing borders

You can put a border round the list and its heading.

▶ Click anywhere in the text.

▶ On the Main Menu bar, click **Edit**. Then click **Select All**. (Alternatively, you could press **Ctrl + A** on the keyboard.)

▶ Click the **Outside Border** button on the Formatting toolbar. Your heading and text will now have a border around it.

Shading the title

In the example (Figure 8.9), we have coloured the heading yellow on a blue background.

▶ Select the title by clicking in the left margin next to it.

▶ Click on the arrow next to the **Font Color** button on the Drawing toolbar, and select a colour for your title.

▶ Now, keeping the heading selected, select **Format** from the Main Menu bar. Then click on **Borders and Shading**.

A dialogue box like the one below will appear:

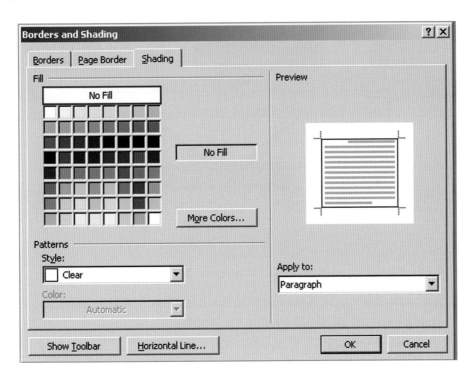

Figure 8.12: Choosing a shading colour

▶ Make sure the **Shading** tab selected.

▶ Choose a shade to go behind your heading, and click **OK**.

▶ When you are happy with your poster, save and print it.

▶ Close your document. To do this you can simply click the **Close** icon in the top right hand corner of the screen.

Chapter 9
Tabs and Tables

Sometimes you might want to produce lists of things arranged in columns. A good way of doing this is to set **Tab stops** and use the **Tab** key to move between these set positions.

Microsoft Word has **default tab positions** which appear as faint marks below the **ruler** underneath the Formatting toolbar.

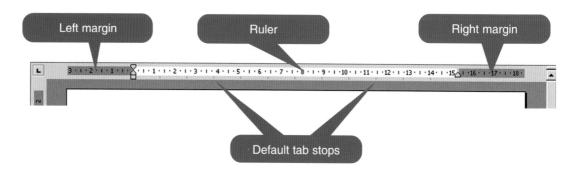

Figure 9.1: The ruler

The default tab stops in Figure 9.1 above are set at intervals of 1.27cm.

> Open a new document and look at the ruler line at the top of the screen. The tabs should be set the same as above.

You are arranging the activities for a forthcoming snowboarding trip, and want to produce lists for yourself to show who has signed up for what activities. This becomes a lot easier if you use the tab stops and the **Tab** key.

Tobogganing	**Skidoo**	Late-night Skiing
Carl	Ed	Laura
Orla	Pina	Alex
Rohan	Sarah	Pete
Sharon	Roberto	May

Figure 9.2

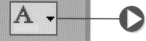

> Type the first word on the list – **Tobogganing**. In Figure 9.2, it is **Bold**, size **14**, and has been coloured red using the **Font Color** button on the Formatting toolbar.

▶ Without using the space bar at all, press the **Tab** key twice and then type in the next list heading. Repeat this for the third heading, before pressing **Enter** twice to leave a space in between the headings and the lists.

▶ Change the font back to size **12** and not bold, before typing in the lists of names.

▶ Play around with your lists until you are happy using the **Tab** key.

You can change the distance between the default tab stops. If you wish to do so, it is easier if you do it *before* you begin typing, as you are about to find out.

▶ Select **Format** from the Main Menu bar. Then click on **Tabs**. A dialogue box like this should appear.

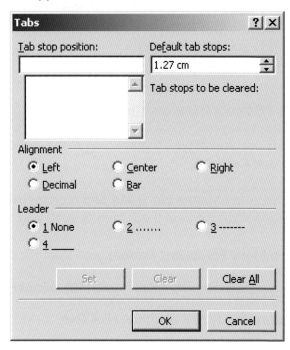

Figure 9.3: Changing default tab stops

▶ Click the up arrow on the right hand side of the **Default tab stops** box until it is set at **2cm**. Then click **OK**.

Instant chaos! When the space between the tab stops was smaller, you needed more tab characters between each name. Now these extra characters need to be deleted.

You can play around with your lists, deleting the extra tab stops using the **Backspace** or **Delete** keys until your lists line up again properly, or you can delete the whole list and start again.

▶ When you are happy with your lists, save and close the document.

Creating your own style of tabs

You can create your own tab stops wherever you want them – and you can also use **leader characters**.

These are the dots that make up the dotted lines that you can see between the items and the prices in the list below:

Hire Prices for Snowboarding/Skiing Equipment

Snowboard & boots (per week) £70.00
Ski-suit (per week) £50.00
Skis & boots (per week)................................£55.00
Lift pass (for a week) £80.00
Skidoo (per hour) £30.00
Toboggan (per hour) £5.00
Ice Skates (per hour) £2.50

Figure 9.4: Custom tabs with leader dots

In a new **Word** document, type the heading of the price list above in **Arial**, size **14 Bold** and **Centred**.

Press **Enter** twice to create a blank line and click the **Align Left** button on the Formatting toolbar. Change the font to size **12** and not bold.

From the Main Menu bar, select **Format**, and then click on **Tabs**.

The dialogue box that appeared before (see Figure 9.3), should be displayed.

In the **Tab Stop Position** box, type **3** and then click **Set**.

Then type **12**, again in the **Tab Stop** Position box.

Click on **Decimal** alignment.

Click on **Leader** option **2**.

Click **Set** and then click **OK**.

Press the **Tab** key to begin the list, entering the items separated by **Tab** and pressing **Enter** at the end of each line.

When you have finished creating your price list, save it as **PriceList** and close your document.

Tip:
Never use the space bar to line things up in columns – Tabs are much easier.

Working with tables

Another way of arranging information in neat columns is to insert a table into your document.

Project: Producing a programme for a winter sports holiday

In this example, you learn how to insert a table into a document and type out a timetable or itinerary like the one shown below:

Programme for Winter Sports Holiday

	Monday	Tuesday	Wednesday	Thursday	Friday	Saturday
10-12	Snowboarding	Snowboarding	Beginners Skiing	Snowboarding	Snowboarding	Beginners Skiing
12-2	LUNCH BREAK					
2-4	Beginners Skiing	Tobogganing	Experienced Skiing	Skidoo	Tobogganing	Experienced Skiing
4-6	Experienced Skiing	Skidoo	Ice Skating	Skidoo	Tobogganing	Snowboarding
6-8	DINNER					
8-late	Apres-Ski	Karaoke	Late-night Skiing	Apres-Ski	Ice Skating	Leaving Party

Figure 9.5

▶ Begin by opening a new document.

▶ Type the heading – **Programme for Winter Sports Holiday**.

▶ Make the heading **Arial**, size **20**, **Bold** and **Centred**.

▶ Press **Enter** twice and change the font back to **Times New Roman**, size **10**, **left aligned** and not bold.

Inserting a table

From the Main Menu bar, select **Table, Insert, Table**. You will see a dialogue box like the one below.

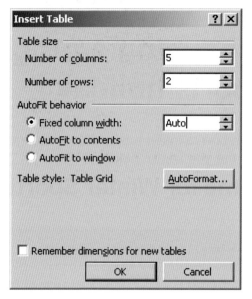

Figure 9.6

▶ Type **7** as the number of columns. (Or use the arrows.)

▶ Press the **Tab** key to move to the next box and enter **7**.

▶ Leave the **Column width** as **Auto** and click the **OK** button.

A table will be inserted into your document like this:

Programme for Winter Sports Holiday

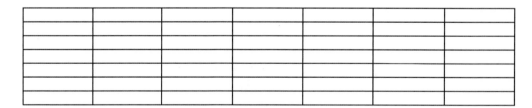

Figure 9.7: An empty table

▶ The cursor should be flashing in the first **cell**, which is in the top left-hand corner of the table.

▶ The first cell is going to remain blank. Press **Tab** to move one cell to the right.

▶ Type **Monday** and then tab to the next cell.

▶ Type **Tuesday, Wednesday**, etc in the cells across the top row.

▶ Press **Tab** to go to the first cell of the second row.

▶ Now fill in the rest of the programme so that it looks like the one below.

Programme for Winter Sports Holiday

	Monday	Tuesday	Wednesday	Thursday	Friday	Saturday
10-12	Snowboarding	Snowboarding	Beginners Skiing	Snowboarding	Snowboarding	Beginners Skiing
12-2	LUNCH BREAK					
2-4	Beginners Skiing	Tobogganing	Experienced Skiing	Skidoo	Tobogganing	Experienced Skiing
4-6	Experienced Skiing	Skidoo	Ice Skating	Skidoo	Tobogganing	Snowboarding
6-8	DINNER					
8-late	Apres-Ski	Karaoke	Late-night Skiing	Apres-Ski	Ice Skating	Leaving Party

Figure 9.8: Your programme so far

Changing the height of the cells

The programme looks rather cramped. It would look better if it was more spread out.

▶ With the cursor in any of the cells of the table, select **Table** from the Main Menu bar. Then click **Select**, **Table**. The whole table will be highlighted.

▶ Select **Table** again from the Main Menu bar. Then click **Table Properties**.

A dialogue box will appear.

▶ Click on the **Row** tab and make entries to match those entered below. The height of each row should be **At least 1cm**.

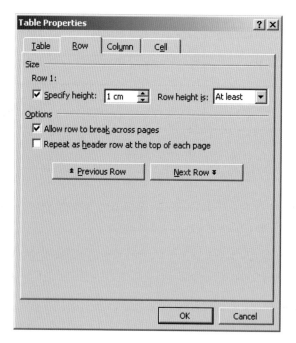

Figure 9.9: The Table Properties dialogue box

▶ Click the **Table** tab. In the **Alignment** section, click the button for **Center** alignment and then click **OK**. This will centre the table between the left and right margins of the page.

Merging cells in a table

If you look at your programme, you will see that the breaks for lunch and dinner occur at the same time every day. You are able to spread the words **Lunch Break** and **Dinner** across several cells to make your table look more balanced.

▶ Drag across the row of cells for the **Lunch Break** period.

▶ From the Main Menu bar, select **Table.** Then select **Merge Cells**.

▶ Click the **Center** and **Bold** buttons on the Formatting toolbar. You can probably make the font bigger too – say size **18**.

▶ Repeat this process for the **Dinner** period of your table.

Formatting text in cells

▶ Click in the first cell of the table and drag across and down until you are in the bottom right corner of the table to select the cells.

▶ Press the **Center** button on the Formatting toolbar. —————————

▶ Click in the left margin beside the top row to select it. Click the **Bold** button on the Formatting toolbar.

You can try out a new way of selecting a column – position the cursor just over the top line of the column until it changes to a downward-pointing arrow. Then click.

▶ Select all the cells in the first column and make them **Bold**.

Shading

You can shade any of the cells in the table.

▶ Click in the left margin beside the top row to select it.

▶ From the Main Menu bar, select **Format**. Then click **Borders and Shading**.

▶ In the dialogue box that appears, click the **Shading** tab.

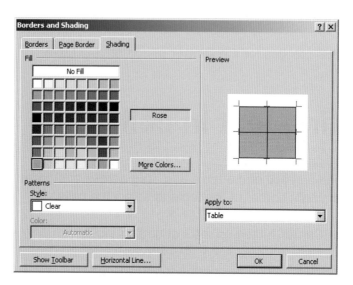

Figure 9.10

▶ Click a colour for the shading – **Rose** has been chosen in the box above – and then click **OK**.

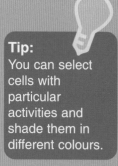
Programme for Winter Sports Holiday

	Monday	Tuesday	Wednesday	Thursday	Friday	Saturday
10-12	Snowboarding	Snowboarding	Beginners Skiing	Snowboarding	Snowboarding	Beginners Skiing
12-2	LUNCH BREAK					
2-4	Beginners Skiing	Tobogganing	Experienced Skiing	Skidoo	Tobogganing	Experienced Skiing
4-6	Experienced Skiing	Skidoo	Ice Skating	Skidoo	Tobogganing	Snowboarding
6-8	DINNER					
8-late	Après-Ski	Karaoke	Late-night Skiing	Après-Ski	Ice Skating	Leaving Party

Figure 9.11

Inserting and deleting rows

Suppose you wanted to insert an extra row above the row for **2-4**.

▶ Click anywhere in the row for **2-4**, then from the Main Menu bar select **Table, Insert, Rows Above**.

▶ Delete the row again by selecting **Table, Delete, Rows**.

▶ If you want to insert an extra row at the end of a table, click in the very last cell (in the bottom right of the table) and press the **Tab** key. You can delete this row again if you wish.

Changing column widths

To change the width of a column, put the pointer over one of the boundary lines separating the cells. When the pointer changes to a double-headed arrow, you can drag the boundary line either way to make the column wider or narrower.

	Monday
10-12	Snowboarding
12-2	
2-4	Beginners

Figure 9.12

Centre text vertically

You have already centred the text *horizontally* so that it appears in the middle of the columns. You are also able to centre it *vertically*, so that the text is right in the middle of the cell.

▶ From the Main Menu bar, select **Table, Select, Table.**

▶ Right-click anywhere in the table and hover over **Cell Alignment**.

▶ Of the nine options given, choose the middle one - **Align Centre**.

▶ Your table should now look like the one in Figure 9.5. Save it and print.

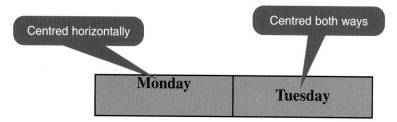

Figure 9.13

Chapter 10
Headers and Footers

Headers and Footers are used in printed documents with the **Header** printed in the top margin and the **Footer** printed in the bottom margin.

You sometimes want something to appear on every page of a document – such as page numbers, the date, a company logo, the file name or the author's name. This is what **Headers** and **Footers** are for.

Project: Create a Header and Footer for Snowboarding Club stationery

As secretary of a snowboarding club, you want stationery that you can use for sending letters to members, printing newsletters and informing members of forthcoming trips or meetings.

You are going to create the letter shown on the following page. To do this, you will be using **Headers** and **Footers**. The **Header and Footer** toolbar is shown below – you won't be using all of the buttons on the toolbar for this particular example, but it is still useful to know what some of them are.

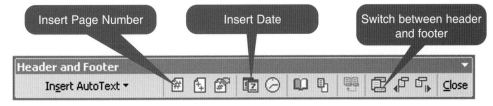

Figure 10.1: The Header and Footer toolbar

15 October 2001

Mr Paul Atkinson
96 Darley Road
King's Norton,
Birmingham
BM64 4DE

Dear Paul,

Please find attached an itinerary detailing the times and activities of the forthcoming snowboarding trip on which you are due to accompany us.

This is being sent out to all of the people who are signed up to go on the trip – some of whom I am sure you already know.

Feel free to contact me if there are any questions you have regarding the week's plans – we will of course be meeting as a group before the planned departure next month.

All the best

Orla May
Secretary
Birmingham Snowboarding Club

Enc.

Birmingham Snowboarding Club, Great Barr Road, Birmingham BM66 2BU

Figure 10.2: The completed letter

Opening the Header box

▶ In a new **Word** document select **View, Header and Footer**. The following Header box and toolbar will appear:

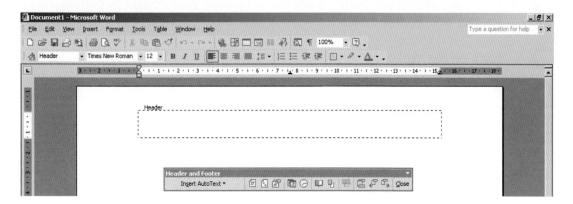

Figure 10.3: The Header box and toolbar

The dotted line will not appear in your document – it indicates the Header area.

You can use the **Tab** key to tab to the centre or right-hand side of the Header or Footer.

▶ Try using the **Header and Footer** toolbar to insert the date in the left-hand side of your Header box.

▶ Now tab to the middle of the Header box and insert a page number.

▶ Finally, tab to the right of the Header box and type in your name. Then close the toolbar and see the effect. You should have something like this:

24/06/2002   1   Carl Grindrod

Figure 10.4: After the Header and Footer toolbar is closed

Inserting WordArt

The special text effect that appears at the top of the letter in Figure 10.2 was created using the **WordArt** button on the Drawing toolbar.

> In a new **Word** document, select **View, Header and Footer** to call up the Header and Footer boxes.

> Click on the **WordArt** button on the Drawing toolbar.

> Choose a text effect from the WordArt Gallery and click **OK**. The effect used in our letter is highlighted in Figure 10.5 below.

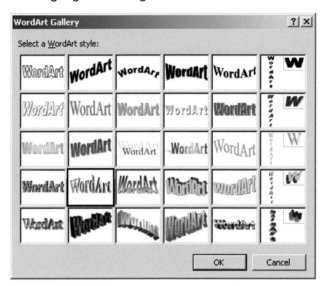

Figure 10.5: The WordArt Gallery

> In the next dialogue box, type the words **Snowboarding Club**. Change the font to **Swiss911 XCm BT** and click **OK**.

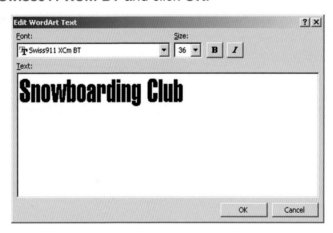

Figure 10.6: Editing the WordArt text

The text will be inserted into your Header box, which will increase in size to accommodate the text.

 Make your text deeper by clicking in it and dragging down on the bottom middle handle to increase its depth. Make it roughly the size of the text in Figure 10.2.

To make any changes to your text, you can use the **WordArt** toolbar. It may appear on the screen when your text is inserted; if not, you can show it by clicking **View**, **Toolbars** and selecting **WordArt** from the list.

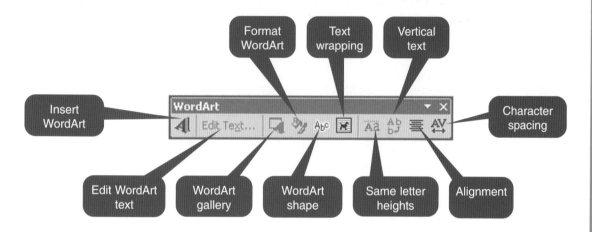

Figure 10.7: The WordArt toolbar

In Figure 10.2, we have changed the shape of the WordArt text.

 Click on the **WordArt Shape** button on the WordArt toolbar. —————————

A pop-up menu will appear with a selection of shapes that can be applied to your text. Your text is currently in the **Triangle Up** style.

 Select the **Inflate** style by clicking on it. Your text should be changed to the new style.

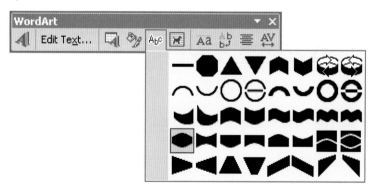

Figure 10.8: Selecting a shape for WordArt

 Insert a clip art image in the right hand side of your Header box.

Inserting a text box

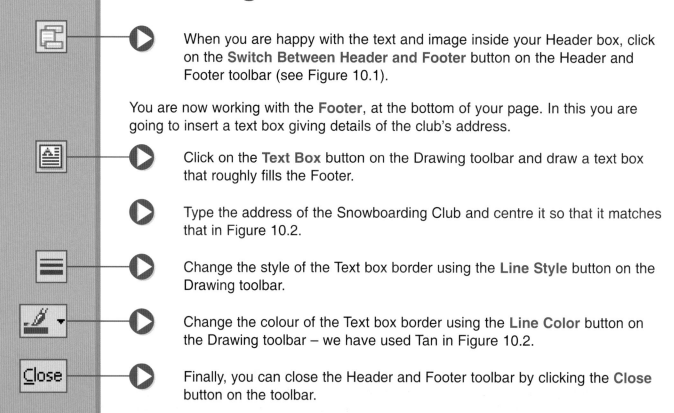

When you are happy with the text and image inside your Header box, click on the **Switch Between Header and Footer** button on the Header and Footer toolbar (see Figure 10.1).

You are now working with the **Footer**, at the bottom of your page. In this you are going to insert a text box giving details of the club's address.

Click on the **Text Box** button on the Drawing toolbar and draw a text box that roughly fills the Footer.

Type the address of the Snowboarding Club and centre it so that it matches that in Figure 10.2.

Change the style of the Text box border using the **Line Style** button on the Drawing toolbar.

Change the colour of the Text box border using the **Line Color** button on the Drawing toolbar – we have used Tan in Figure 10.2.

Finally, you can close the Header and Footer toolbar by clicking the **Close** button on the toolbar.

Inserting a field

After closing the Header and Footer toolbar, the insertion point will appear underneath your Header. You can now insert today's date in this position in a special way – using a **Field**.

From the Main Menu bar, select **Insert, Field**.

In the dialogue box select **Date and Time** in the **Categories** box, and **Date** in the **Field names** box. A list of possible **Date formats** will appear in the **Field Properties** column.

Select the format d MMMM yyyy, as highlighted in Figure 10.9.

Click **OK**. The date will appear beneath your header.

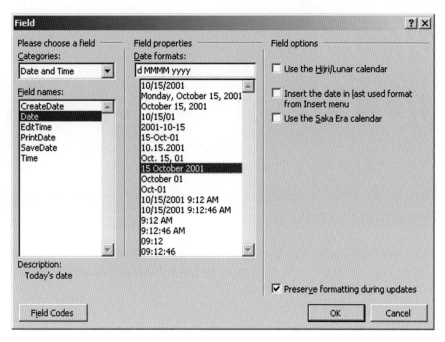

Figure 10.9: Formatting the Date field

With the Date field inserted, you can now type out the rest of the letter.

▶ Press **Enter** twice after your date and enter in the remaining text. The letter shown is typed in standard business format, with all paragraphs aligned to the left and one blank line between paragraphs. The letters **Enc.** at the end of the letter indicate that there should be an enclosure – in this case a programme for the winter sports holiday.

▶ When you have finished, save the letter as **snowboarding.doc**.

Chapter 11
Creating Business Cards

In this chapter you will learn how to design and print business cards, tickets or labels. You can buy special perforated card to print them on, or you can just print your cards on thin card and cut them up.

Project: Create a sheet of business cards

You have been asked to design and create a sheet of business cards for the Managing Director of a book wholesaler. The final set of cards should look something like this:

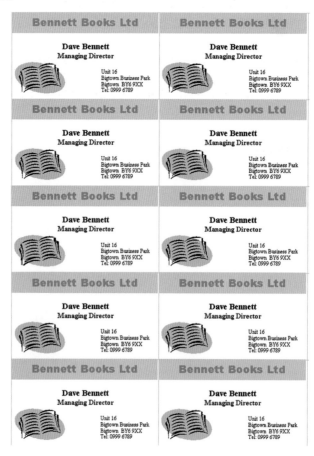

Figure 11.1: A sheet of business cards

Setting up the margins

▶ In a new **Word** document, select **File, Page Setup.**

▶ Measure the margins of your chosen stationery carefully, or use the dimensions shown in Figure 11.2.

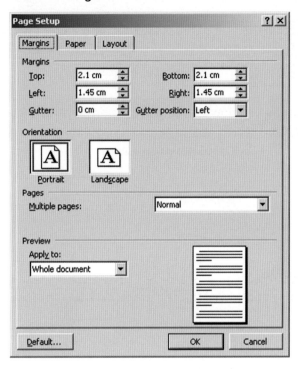

Figure 11.2: Setting up the margins

▶ Click the **Paper** tab, make sure that the paper size is set to **A4** and click **OK**.

▶ Save the blank document as **BusinessCards.doc**.

Setting up the grid

▷ Measure the dimensions of the cards in your chosen stationery. In this example we will be producing ten cards on the page, each **9cm** by **5.1cm**.

Draw ▾

▷ Click **Draw** on the Drawing toolbar and select **Grid**.

▷ Set the grid dimensions of the business cards as shown in Figure 11.3 and click **OK**.

Make sure **Snap objects to grid** is not selected

This option should be selected

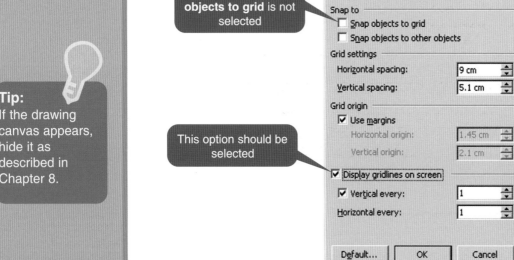

Figure 11.3: Setting the grid

Creating the business cards

▶ Use the **Text box** button from the Drawing toolbar to insert a text box in the top of your first grid box. Make it the same width as the box and about a quarter of its depth.

▶ Making sure the text is **centred**, type in the company name. In our example it is **Arial Black**, size **18**. Then use the **Font Color** button to colour the text green, and the **Fill Color** button to give the text box a light grey background.

Figure 11.4: Using a text box within the grid

▶ Select the text box and use the **Line Color** button to select **No Line**. The text box border will disappear.

▶ Now draw a second text box below the first and with the text again centred, enter the next line in **Times New Roman,** size **14**, **bold**. Then enter the title line changing the size to **12**. Remove the text box border. Make sure you leave enough room below this text box for the clip art image you are going to insert.

▶ Make sure neither text box is selected and select **Insert**, **Picture**, **Clip Art** from the Main Menu bar. In the Insert Clip Art Task pane, type **books** in the **Search for** box and click on **Search**. Select any suitable clip. Click on it and it will be inserted into the first box in your grid.

▶ Right-click anywhere in the clip art, and select **Format Picture**. Select the **Layout** tab and click **In front of text**, then **OK**. Now it should have white handles, which allows you to move it wherever you want.

▶ Move your image into the bottom left of the grid box and size it to fit.

▶ Finally, enter another text box and type in the address and phone number for the company. Make it **Times New Roman**, size **9**.

Warning:
If **Snap objects to grid** is selected, you will only be able to draw a text box that exactly fills the gridlines. That is why you de-selected this option in Figure 11.3.

Reminder:
Copy the text from Figure 11.1

Tip:
If you can't see the picture after it is inserted, it is probably hidden behind the top text box. Drag the text box aside to expose it. (You can replace the text box to its proper position when you have finished with the clip art).

Copying the business card

▶ Holding down the **Shift** key, select all of the separate items in your grid box individually. Then right-click inside the business card and select **Grouping**, **Group**. This ensures that all the objects on the card will be treated as a single object.

▶ Select **Draw**, **Grid** again. This time select **Snap objects to grid**, before clicking **OK**.

▶ Use the **Zoom** button to change the view to 50%. This will enable you to see most of the sheet.

`50%` ▾

▶ By holding down the **Ctrl** key and dragging, you can now copy the card 9 times to the rest of the page. It will snap into place as soon as you approach the correct area and you should end up with a sheet of 10 cards.

Resetting the grid

▶ Before you start working on another document select **Draw**, **Grid** for a final time and de-select **Snap objects to grid** and **Display gridlines on screen**, before clicking **OK**.

▶ Check that the grid size has been set back to its original settings. This is usually .32cm both horizontally and vertically.

Tip:
If next time you use the screen it looks like graph paper, you have forgotten to remove the gridlines.

Chapter 12
Mail Merge

You will have undoubtedly received, at some time, a letter informing you that you have won £1 million! Letters like this, that use huge databases of names to produce what seems to be a highly personalised letter with your name on it, are created using a **mail merge**. Mail merges can also be used to produce labels or print directly onto envelopes.

Project: Produce personalised letters for the Snowboarding Club

In Chapter 10 you created a letter that was set on Snowboarding Club stationery. Suppose that you need to send that particular letter to everybody else who is going on the trip that you have organised. You will also need to print address labels for the envelopes.

Creating the letters

There are six steps involved in setting up a mail merge:

Step 1: Selecting the type of document you are working on.

Step 2: Setting up and displaying your document.

Step 3: Selecting recipients – opening or creating the list of names and addresses to whom the document is being sent.

Step 4: Writing your letter.

Step 5: Previewing the letters.

Step 6: Completing the merge.

Step 1: Selecting the type of document you are working on.

▶ Open the letter you created in Chapter 10 – it should be saved as **snowboarding.doc**.

▶ From the Main Menu bar, select **Tools, Letters and Mailings, Mail Merge Wizard**. The Mail Merge Task pane should appear on the right of the screen.

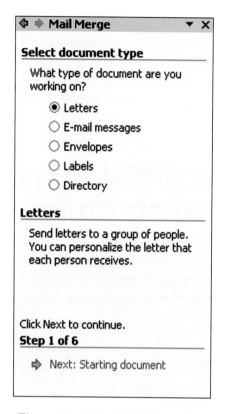

▶ Make sure you have selected **Letters** as the document type you are working with.

▶ Now click on **Next: Starting document** at the bottom of the Task pane. This will take you on to step 2.

Figure 12.1: The Mail Merge Task pane – Step 1

Step 2: Select starting document – setting up your letter

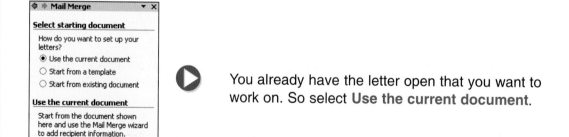

▶ You already have the letter open that you want to work on. So select **Use the current document**.

Figure 12.2: Mail Merge – Step 2

▶ Click on **Next: Select recipients** to move on to step 3.

Step 3: Selecting recipients

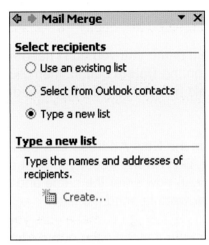

Figure 12.3: Mail Merge – Step 3

 You don't currently have any lists or contacts, so you need to create your own. Select the **Type a new list** option and click on **Create** in the section that appears. A dialogue box like the one below should appear.

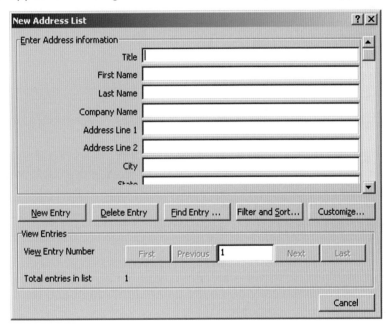

Figure 12.4: Creating a new address list

Tip:
You can press the **Tab** key to move from one box to the next.

 Enter the name and address from the letter that you have on screen. Enter the post code of the address in the box that is entitled **ZIP Code**. This is simply the American equivalent of our post code.

You will have left a lot of the boxes in the dialogue box blank – for example **Company name** and **State**. You can delete these unneeded boxes from your records.

▶ Click the **Customize** button in the dialogue box. A further dialogue box will appear.

▶ Click on the first field name that you don't need – **Company Name**. With this selected, click on the **Delete** button, then click **Yes** to confirm. Repeat this for the other field names that you don't need for your address list. Click **OK**.

▶ Now you are back in the **New Address List** box. Click on **New Entry** and the boxes will clear. Don't worry about your first entry – it is automatically saved for you. You can now enter the name and address of a second person to whom you want to send the letter.

Reminder:
Use the ones in Figure 12.18 if you wish.

▶ Fill in the details for your second person and click **New Entry**. Repeat this until you have entered 5 or 6 addresses for your list. Then click **Close**. Another dialogue box will appear:

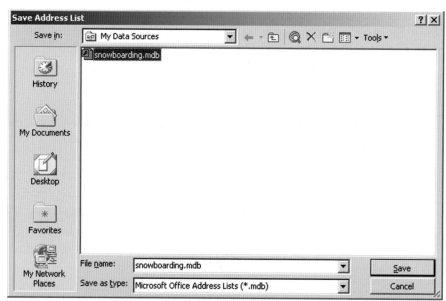

Figure 12.5: Saving your address list

Your address list will automatically be saved as an **.mdb** database file in the **My Data Sources** area of your computer.

▶ Save your address list as **snowboarding.mdb**.

When you have saved your address list, a further box will appear – the **Mail Merge Recipients** box. This allows you to view your completed list of names and addresses and make any amendments – for example you may want to arrange them in a particular order, or perhaps change one of the addresses.

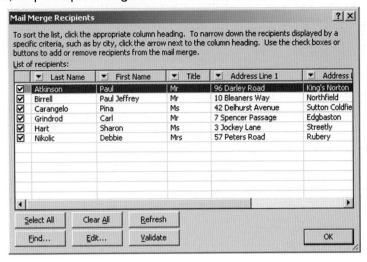

Figure 12.6: The Mail Merge Recipients box

Suppose in the example above you wanted to delete **Jeffrey** in the name **Paul Jeffrey Birrell**.

▶ Select the whole entry by clicking anywhere along the line that contains his information. Then click on the **Edit** button.

▶ The box that appears is the same as the original **New Address List** box, except it is now full of the information you stored in it. By selecting Paul Birrell's name in the Mail Merge Recipients box, you are ensuring that it is his information that appears on screen. Now drag across the name **Jeffrey** to select it, and press the **Backspace** key. The name will disappear.

▶ Click on **Close** and you are taken back to the Mail Merge Recipients box, in which the amended name appears. Now click **OK** and you are ready to move on to step 4 of your mail merge.

▶ At the bottom of the Task pane, click on **Next: Write your letter**.

Tip:
If at any point you wish to return to a previous step of your mail merge, you can do so by clicking the back arrow in the top left of the mail merge Task pane. Alternatively, click on **Previous** at the bottom of the Task pane and it will take you back to the last step that you completed.

⇐ Previous: Select recipients

Step 4:   Write your letter

Figure 12.7: Mail Merge – Step 4

You have already written your letter. However, you do want to add recipient information, in the form of the names and addresses you saved in the previous step. Also, you want to add a greeting line so that all of your letters don't say **Dear Paul** like the original letter.

▶ In your original letter, highlight the name and address you entered beginning **Mr Paul Atkinson** and ending with the postcode.

▶ Now click on **Address Block...** in the Task pane. A dialogue box will appear:

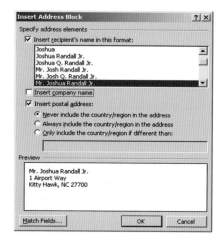

Figure 12.8: Inserting an Address Block

▶ Choose a suitable format for the recipient's name and set the other options as above. Press **OK**.

▶ With the insertion point positioned after «AddressBlock»», press **Enter** to create a blank line.

Now highlight the first line of the letter – **Dear Paul** – and click on **Greeting line** in the Task pane.

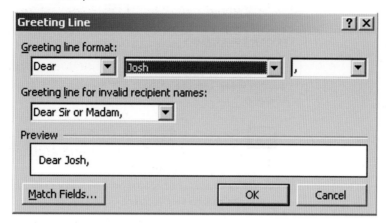

Figure 12.9: Selecting a greeting line

 Select the Greeting line format that uses just the first name, and then click **OK**. With the insertion point after **««GreetingLine»»** in your letter, press **Enter**.

The screen should now be looking something like this:

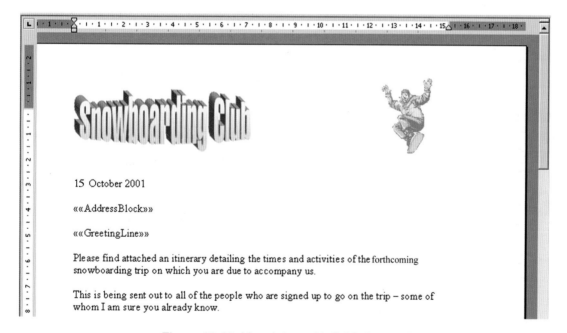

Figure 12.10: Your letter with fields inserted

With your letter completed, you are now able to preview and personalise each recipient's letter.

 Click **Next: Preview your letters** at the bottom of the Task pane.

Step 5: Previewing your letters

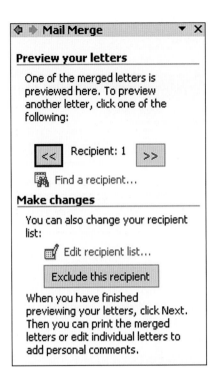

Figure 12.11: Mail Merge – Step 5

 You should see the preview of the first of your letters, with the address block and the greeting line inserted as you selected. Click on the arrow button to the right of **Recipient: 1** to preview the other letters.

You may notice that in the address block for each letter, the post code appears on the same line as the city. You will want to change this to ensure that the post code appears on a line of its own – you will be doing this during the final step of the merge.

 Click **Next: Complete the merge** to move on to the last step of your merge.

Step 6: Completing the merge

You are now ready to complete the merge and produce your letters. However, first you must edit your individual letters to ensure that the post codes are properly positioned in the text.

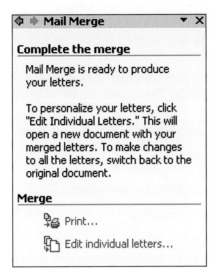

Figure 12.12: Completing the merge – Step 6

▶ Click on **Edit individual letters**.

▶ In the Merge to New Document dialogue box select **All** and click **OK**.

▶ A new document automatically opens containing all your letters. This document will be called **Letters1**, and you can now scroll down through each letter individually.

▶ In your first letter, press **Enter** immediately before the post code to send it to a new line. Repeat this for the other letters, before saving the file and finally printing. You have now completed your mail merge. The letters can be printed.

Creating mailing labels

You can now create the labels to stick on the envelopes. For this, you can use the same name and address data that you have already stored as **snowboarding.mdb** and choose to create labels instead of Form letters.

▶ Click the **New Blank Document** button on the Standard toolbar.

▶ From the Main Menu bar, select **Tools**, **Letters and Mailings**, **Mail Merge Wizard**. The Mail Merge Task pane again appears.

▶ Select the **Labels** option before clicking on **Next: Starting document**.

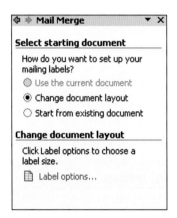

Figure 12.13: Changing document layout

▶ With **Change document layout** selected as in Figure 12.13, click on **Label options** to choose the size of your labels.

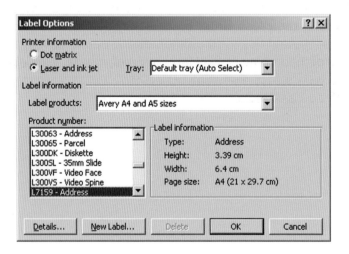

Figure 12.14: Choosing label size

▶ Select your own size of label from the options shown in Figure 12.14, and click **OK**. A grid of label outlines will appear in your document.

▶ Click on **Next: Select recipients** at the bottom of the Task pane.

▶ You want to use the same list of data that you used previously in setting up your mail merge. With **Use an existing list** selected, click on **Browse.**

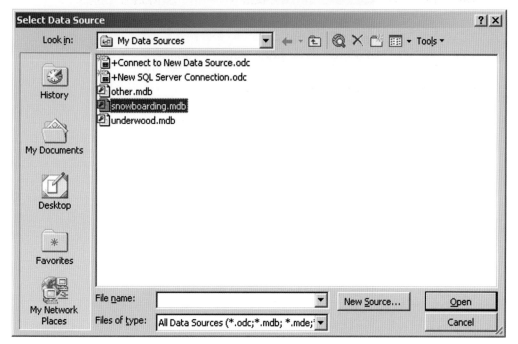

Figure 12.15: Selecting a data source

▶ In the dialogue box, select the file **snowboarding.mdb** that you created earlier in the chapter and click **Open**. The Mail Merge Recipients box will open showing the information you saved earlier – simply click **OK**.

▶ With the insertion point in the first box in your grid, you are ready to begin putting your data onto the labels. Click on **Next: Arrange your labels** at the bottom of the Task pane.

When performing the actual mail merge, you inserted an **Address block** into your letter. However, you then had to edit the address block because it automatically positioned the post code on the same line as the city. This time you are going to insert the data fields manually.

 Click on the **More items** option. The dialogue box below will appear:

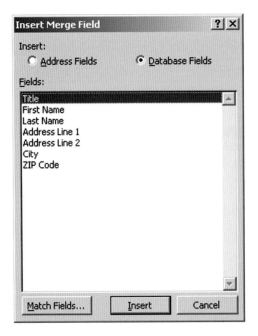

Figure 12.16

The Insert Merge Fields box presents you with the fields that you had previously saved in your database when performing the mail merge. You want to insert all of these fields into your labels.

 With **Title** selected, click on **Insert** to insert the field into the first label. Select and insert every other field in the dialogue box. When you have inserted ZIP Code, click on **Close** (which once you have inserted the first field replaces the **Cancel** button in the figure above).

Your fields currently have no spacing between them, so if you tried to preview your labels now they would look like the one below.

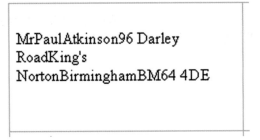

Figure 12.17

94

▶ Insert a space between «**Title**» and «**First_Name**» by placing the insertion point directly after «**Title**» and pressing the space bar. Repeat this to insert a space between «**First_Name**» and «**Last_Name**».

▶ Insert a line break after «**Last_Name**» by placing the insertion point directly after it and pressing **Enter**. Repeat this to insert line breaks at the end of every other field in your label apart from after the last line of the address, the post code.

▶ Once you have arranged your data fields into the right format, click on the **Update all labels** button to ensure that all of your labels have the same format.

Update all Labels

▶ Now you are ready to preview your labels – click on **Next: Preview your labels** at the bottom of the Task pane. They should look like this:

Mr Paul Atkinson 96 Darley Road King's Norton Birmingham BM64 4DE	Ms Pina Carangelo 42 Delhurst Avenue Sutton Coldfield Birmingham BM45 8UH	Mr Carl Grindrod 7 Spencer Passage Edgbaston Birmingham BM22 1QA
Ms Sharon Hart 3 Jockey Lane Streetly Birmingham BM19 6GT	Mrs Debbie Nikolic 57 Peters Road Rubery Birmingham BM52 9RN	Mr Paul Birrell 10 Bleaners Way Northfield Birmingham BM48 9OL

Figure 12.18: Your mailing labels

▶ Click on **Next: Complete the merge** to go to the final stage of creating your labels.

▶ In the final Task pane, click on **Edit individual labels**. In the **Merge to new document** dialogue box that appears, make sure **All** is selected before clicking **OK**. This creates a new document containing your actual labels with the names and addresses on, probably called **Labels2.doc**. You are now able to make any changes you think need making before saving the labels.

▶ Save your labels as **Labels2.doc**. Now print them, making sure that you have label stationery loaded in the printer.

Index